FATHER'S VINEYARD

CINDY STEINBECK

Published by Voice In The Vineyard Ministries

Copyright 2023 by Cindy Steinbeck

All rights reserved. Unless specifically noted, no part of this publication may be reproduced, stored in a retrieval system, or transmitted, in any form or by any means, electronic, mechanical, photocopying, recording, or otherwise, without the prior written permission of Cindy Steinbeck.

Scripture quotations are from the ESV® Bible (The Holy Bible, English Standard Version®), copyright © 2001 by Crossway, a publishing ministry of Good News Publishers. Used by permission. All rights reserved. The ESV text may not be quoted in any publication made available to the public by a Creative Commons license. The ESV may not be translated in whole or in part into any other language.

Scripture quotations taken from the (NASB®) New American Standard Bible®, Copyright © 1960, 1971, 1977, 1995, 2020 by The Lockman Foundation. Used by permission. All rights reserved. *lockman.org*

*Honoring God, the vinedresser,
Father of the one true vine, and His Spirit.*

*Servant Howie Steinbeck, my father, the vinedresser,
who unwrapped many images herein.*

*Servant Bill Diekelman, who read and re-read Father's
Vineyard, guiding me with clarity and passion for the vine.
Bill's undeniable love for those who will be further connected
to the vine reflects the vinedresser's passion for all.*

Servant Beth Moore, for Chasing Vines, *your presence in
Steinbeck Vineyards, and for your tears of passion for the
message of the vineyard, the vinedresser, and the vine.*

*Servants Ron & Becki Beers for encouraging me to write
words of hope from my story, not apart from it.*

CONTENTS

INTRODUCTION vii
JESUS' I AM STATEMENTS x

Chapter 1 CONNECTED 1
          Study 1: The Vine And The Branches 2
          Study 2: Abide In The Vine 12
          Study 3: Rooted In Christ 20
          Study 4: The Sap—The Lifeblood 35
          Study 5: Healing In Christ 44
          Study 6: Growing In Christ 56

Chapter 2 PROCESS WITH PURPOSE 69
          Study 7: The Vinedresser And The Vine 71
          Study 8: The Trellis System 83
          Study 9: Training Young Branches 96
          Study 10: Thinning Shoots And Fruit 107
          Study 11: Pruning 121

Chapter 3 THE GIFTS 135
          Study 12: The Fruit 136
          Study 13: Harvest 149
          Study 14: The Wine—The Fermentation Process 163
          Study 15: The Wine—Taste, Smell, And See 174
          Study 16: The Fellowship 183

Chapter 4 THE VINEDRESSER'S CALL 193
          Study 17: Terroir 195
          Study 18: Balance 203
          Study 19: Connecting 216
          Study 20: Abiding 231
          Study 21: Multiplying Growth 242

TERMS & CONCEPTS 253

INTRODUCTION

My father, Howie Steinbeck, planted each vine in Steinbeck Vineyards. He tended those vines as owner and farmer. He cultivated among his vines, watching each one grow and produce mature fruit for fine wine. He's known as a vinedresser. As a vinedresser, he worked and as a vinedresser, he directed workers to care for the vines.

His grandson, my son, serves as vinedresser today. Ryan studied under and worked with and for his grandpa. From the time he was two years old he knew one thing: he wanted to grow wine grapes with his grandpa. He respects his grandpa and admires the work he accomplished as he built and tended Steinbeck Vineyards. He accepted the vinedresser role

His grandson, my son-in-law, crafts Steinbeck wines from a small percentage of fruit from our vines. Bryan studied music and theology in college, planning to continue with school to serve in full-time ministry. His detour for a year of rest prior to attending grad school, led to a career in wine making. He journeyed to Tasmania, Australia for 4 years and then back to Paso Robles to work under our winemaker for another four.

While grandpa doesn't actively tend the vines or make our wines, his heart cheers Ryan and Bryan on. He still looks at the vineyard as one who planted each vine. He takes pride in their work and assists when he can.

I worked under dad too, for 15 years, farming vines with him. I retired from my ministry career as a Director of Christian Education, moved home to the vineyard and continued to feed my love for the soil, the vines, and farming with my father. Awaking early, I'd read Jesus' words and then jump on my John Deere tractor to work the fields or my 4-wheeler to irrigate the vines.

I continue to watch these men as well as draw from my own years farming. Jesus' declared, "I am the true vine, and my Father is the vinedresser" and "I am the vine; you are the branches. Whoever abides in me and I in him, he it is that bears much fruit, for apart from me you can do nothing." Those "I am" statements invite a deep dive into Jesus' why!

Hundreds of thousands vines grow in the land, roots seeking water, branches growing in the sunlight. While the vinedresser sees the vineyard as a whole, he sees and cares for one vine at a time. As we journey together, you'll see many vines in Steinbeck Vineyards. Our focus is the vine but more importantly, one vine, Jesus.

Our heavenly Father invites us to focus on His son, the one true vine. *Father's Vineyard* reflects that focal point, Jesus, the vine of His father. Father's words and the vine's words call us into a deeper understanding of our connection with Him. Further, you and I will connect through His word and desire a deeper connection with those around us—that is the way of the vine and His father.

Thousands of branches exist in Steinbeck Vineyards, and thousands of branches of the one true vine exist in this world. *Father's Vineyard* unfolds factors common to all branches and invites you, an individual, to be held and cherished for your unique gifts. *Father's Vineyard* prayerfully challenges you to mature in faith and bear the fruit that grows from abiding in the vine.

Join me in my Jeep on a tour of Steinbeck Vineyards, my classroom as we unfold these burning questions, Why did Jesus proclaim, "I am the true vine my father is the vinedresser," "I am the vine; you are the branches, abide in me," and "I am the root?"

JESUS' **I AM** STATEMENTS

"I am" statements are not images, metaphor, or analogy. Through them, Jesus declared himself to be the great "I am" and connected himself to God's work through Moses. Jesus would not have been hung on a cross had he said, "I am one true vine of many true vines" or "I am like a vine" or "I am one way of many ways." He is the great "I am."

Images I unfold can be powerful likenesses. I have seen many through my work in Steinbeck Vineyards, but they are only images. We must separate, in honor of Christ, my images, from his declaration of "I am the true vine."

CHAPTER 1

CONNECTED

Holding my work in your hands connects you and me. We'll be connected further as I make image-driven correlations of vines to branches and Jesus. Jesus declared his intimate dwelling within us, branches of the true vine, connecting him to us and us to one another.

In this chapter, we'll explore the basics of the vines, branches, and seasons, laying a foundation for our journey together. We will jump right into the heart of the vine story by diving into the rich meaning of being grafted as a branch into a vine.

The roots of the vine invite us to focus our attention on Jesus' "I am" declaration, "I am the root and the descendant of David, the bright morning star" (Revelation 22:16b). Roots draw in nutrients and water as well as provide stability and structure — Jesus is all that and more for us.

We'll travel inside a single vine, likening the sap flow to Jesus' blood. Sustenance, growth, and healing will be explored as sap flows from our profound "abiding" relationship, grafted into the one true vine.

STUDY 1: THE VINE AND THE BRANCHES

Why did Jesus say, "I am the vine; you are the branches. Whoever abides in me and I in him, he it is that bears much fruit, for apart from me you can do nothing" (John 15:5)? I've prayed, begging God to show me the answers to this critical question year after year. Over the past years, God has worked through our 500-acre vineyard that serves as my classroom to teach me insights I'm excited to share with you.

First, I must tell you about my Jeep! If you're imagining a pristine, well-polished Jeep Willys restored to its original 1958 glory, don't. Envision rust and chipped or worn paint. A small chunk of whittled wood rests between the hood and frame to help stop the rattling. The tow hitch rattles too. To curb that, my dad shoved a worn-out glove between the metal pieces and tightened the mechanism.

We launch our tour, encouraging questions. You might think to ask, "How old is this Jeep?" "Does it still run?" "Are you related to John Steinbeck?" Sometimes questions sound more like statements. "This thing still runs?" One of the unique statements I've chuckled about over time is, "Disney pays a lot of money to make things look like this!" Shoulder to shoulder, we sit together, in our small rustic vehicle, inside my 500-acre classroom — Steinbeck Vineyards.

Three hundred thousand grape vines surround us, planted in the soil of our particular place in Paso Robles, CA, located precisely halfway between San Francisco and Los Angeles. The beautiful Pacific Ocean lies 30 winding miles west, with waves crashing on the beautiful shoreline of California's Central Coast. The Santa Lucia Mountain range separates Paso from the ocean, providing perfect temperatures and flowing wind in the morning and evening.

Here's a little perspective of our little spot on the map in the enormous state of California. An acre is equivalent to a football field — 500 acres, 500 adjacent football fields. Imagine stunning hilltop views as far as the eye can see, rolling hills, and subtle to drastic elevation changes. My dad shared his dream to build a house with his date in 1957. Dad married mom in 1959. His vision and promise were fulfilled in 1999. Mom designed their beautiful home; dad served as general contractor as they watched their dream come true. Family and friends gather to celebrate or mourn, always enjoying both food and fellowship.

The other hilltop overlooking our vineyards and the entire Paso Robles area is host to three oak trees. One beautifully shaped giant oak is the signature tree for the Chamber of Commerce of the City of Paso Robles. The Spanish name, El Paso De Robles, means the pass of the oaks, so, looking for the perfect tree, the Chamber team settled on this one.

The branches of my favorite old oak tree twist toward the sky and ground, inviting us to imagine the sights it has seen over the 300-plus years it's been rooted in the harsh soils. We gaze at the stunning heart in the tree, formed over the years by a twisted branch. My cousin spotted it through a sweet photo I posted on Facebook. I thought I was sharing a photo of mom and dad walking hand in hand toward the giant oak on their 55th anniversary. He had eyes to see, so today, we see the heart every time we travel to the highest point on the ranch, lovingly named, Oma's Hill.

Three hundred sixty-degree views wow me whenever I drive a Jeep tour group to the top of Oma's Hill! You gasp and declare wow as you see these sights for the first time. Hills north and south, mountains to the west, flat land to the east, it's no wonder grandpa Frank and grandma Rosie (my father's grandparents) chose this land for their family home and ranch. Cattle and grain were the perfect crops for these rolling hills. I imagine their children playing in the same creeks that run with winter rains becoming a puddle-jumping, dam-building playground for me and my grandchildren!

The Vine & The Branches

Jesus knows this land—he spoke it into being. Jesus knows every aspect of a grapevine—He created them.

Grapevines appear to the eye as a reasonably simple plant—the trunk, branches, leaves, and fruit. Nutrients and water flow from the root, through the trunk, to the branches, leaves, and fruit. Leaves absorb sunlight and convert it to energy in the form of carbohydrates. We can see these various vine components, but what can't we see?

We cannot see the roots stretching deep into the earth. Roots provide stability for the plant we see above ground. Roots draw water and nutrients from the soil, transferring them via the sap throughout the vine and branches.

We cannot see sap, the lifeblood of the vine, flowing at all times through the plant. The sap's work is to carry the nutrients and water to the plant's cells.

We cannot see the millions of cells that make up every vine. The cells in the trunk and older branches are firmer and woodier and, as a whole, provide stability, structure, and a boundary to the sap that flows back and forth through the trunk. The cells in the shoots are younger and more supple, allowing the branches to wave effortlessly in the wind.

Stopping the Jeep, I hop out and cut a shoot off the cordon. Holding that shoot in my hand, I show you a leaf, highlighting where the leaf is attached to the shoot. At that place, there is a bud. Inside each bud, tightly wound, is the following year's growth, including the shoots, leaves, and fruit. Look here, and here, and here. A bud grows at the base of each leaf. We pause to grasp the number of leaves and buds on 300,000 vines.

I invite you to imagine how much fruit could be grown from all those buds. Making my first scripture connection to us as fruit-bearing branches, grown out of a little bud I quote, "We are his workmanship, created in Christ Jesus for good works, which God prepared beforehand, that we should walk in them" (Ephesians 2:10).

We sit in silence, pausing and pondering the richness. Breaking the silence, I point out another fascinating fact—one bud develops next year's growth, the shoot I'm holding was grown this year, last year's wood is also visible, and then, by counting the wounds, we can count each year in the life of the plant. We can trace each year of the vine's life back, from the plant's growth, to the trunk that was once a supple branch! I wave my hand, gesturing over the entire vineyard.

The complexity of grapevines pairs beautifully with Jesus'

words, "I am the vine; you are the branches." Scientists have discovered a lot about vines and branches, but they don't know everything about the intricacies of a grapevine. I'm a long-time student of vines and branches, and I've studied science, and I've asked questions of the vinedresser. Jesus knows everything about complex vines and branches!

The disciples walked the earth with the man, Jesus, the creator of the grapevine. He spoke it into being. Jesus knows. Jesus knows every intimate, intricate, complex detail of the vine and our lives as branches abiding in Him. Everything modern science has discovered and has yet to discover about vines and branches, Jesus knows.

Jesus knows every intimate, intricate, complex detail of your life as a branch in Him.

Jesus spoke, "I am the vine," in the context of vines and vineyards surrounding villages and cities. As the disciples walked with Jesus from place to place, I imagine them pausing to nibble a sweet grape ripe for harvest in the fall. Jesus likely talked about the strength of the trunk, the depth of the roots, and that the shoots growing this year produce buds for the following year.

I imagine Jesus connecting the dots of the intricacies of the vine and branches for the disciples many times over the three years He walked with them. I envision Jesus, long before He made His profound declaration of His intimate, abiding relationship with us, leading vineyard tours for His disciples.

The disciples were unaware that Jesus was making His way to the cross when He spoke, "I am the vine; you are the branches, abide." They could not have known just how hard abiding would be as they watched their friend falsely accused, beaten, hung on the cross, and buried in a tomb. We know the story of the cross and grave from the fulfillment side of the story, with a full view. We know Jesus' story ends with the resurrection. We know our joy-filled, pain-filled stories end with the resurrection.

The vine calls us to grasp hold and trust that our intimate connection to Him means growing and living life, now, here. Being intimately connected to Him means life now and life eternal.

Grasp hold and trust that we are intimately connected to Jesus, and that means growth and life. Here. Now.

Jesus declared, "I have said these things to keep you from falling away" (John 16:1). What are "these things"? Jesus speaks of being connected to him as a branch to the vine. His words, "Abide in me," are paramount. Jesus' other words about pruning, bearing fruit, and asking God for anything in Jesus' name have rich implications for our lives too. The disciples needed these words; we need these words. Why? By God's holy design, we crave connection! Connected as a branch to the vine keeps us from falling away amid life's challenges and seasons.

Seasons in The Vineyard

Aspects of life in the vineyard we cannot control are the seasons and the weather. You nod your head in agreement. That's farming! We're bouncing around in my Jeep on an unseasonably cool August day. Fretting about rain during the fall harvest cannot change one thing, nor can worrying about a later-than-average bud break in the spring.

Acknowledging we are not in control, we worship God, creator of the seasons. "And God said, 'Let there be lights in the expanse of the heavens to separate the day from the night. And let them be for signs and for seasons, and for days and years, and let them be lights in the expanse of the heavens to give light upon the earth.' And it was so" (Genesis 1:14-15).

Solomon wisely, poetically, wrote, "For everything, there is a season, and a time for every matter under heaven. A time to be born, and a time to die; a time to plant, and a time to pluck up what is planted" (Ecclesiastes 3:1-2).

For everything here in the vineyard, there is a season. Over the winter months, we prune the vines so that prime fruit will grow in the spring and mature over the summer. The flurry of fall harvest ushers in great joy and celebration! Winter equals rest; spring is a time of rapid growth; summer is a time for maturing; fall means picking fruit and making wine.

Seasons in life may be more complex and more challenging to identify. One of the hardest lessons I've learned by observing my lack of control over the seasons in nature is that I'm not in control during many of the seasons in life. Grief has been introduced by the unexpected death of someone I love. A painful season of healing has perhaps been thrown my way by trauma beyond my control.

The disciples of Jesus wanted to know the times or seasons, likely so they could control the uncontrollable. Ponder their conversation,

> So when they had come together, they asked him, "Lord, will you at this time restore the kingdom to Israel?" He

said to them, "It is not for you to know times or seasons that the Father has fixed by his own authority. But you will receive power when the Holy Spirit has come upon you, and you will be my witnesses in Jerusalem and in all Judea and Samaria, and to the end of the earth." And when he had said these things, as they were looking on, he was lifted up, and a cloud took him out of their sight. Acts 1:6-9

The season of Jesus' time with His disciples on earth ended in an instant when He ascended into heaven. Imagine what they'd been through over those trying days, the season of their Lord being sacrificed! Jesus' call to abide was spoken on the path to the Garden of Gethsemane.

The disciples listened to Jesus' beautiful, agony-filled prayer. They saw tears and blood roll down His face. They watched Jesus mercifully heal a guard whose ear Peter had severed off with a sword in a futile attempt to thwart Jesus' arrest. Their Lord was falsely accused, beaten, and forced to carry His cross down the long path to Calvary.

Peter, three times, denied His Lord. Helpless to save and unaware that Jesus didn't need them to save Him, they could only watch with bleeding hearts. They witnessed the perfect lamb of God as He fulfilled all righteousness by dying a sinner's death on the cross. These mercy-filled words may not have been at the forefront of their minds during this season, "Come to me all you who are weary and heavy laden, and I will give you rest. Take my yoke upon you, and learn from me, for I am gentle and lowly in heart, and you will find rest for your souls. For my yoke is easy, and my burden is light" (Matthew 11:28-30).

Jesus' final question pierced their very being, "My God, my God, why have you forsaken me?" (Matthew 27:46b) Jesus' final words wounded their confused, broken hearts, "It is finished!" The End! Season over!

The women placed Jesus' bloodied, beaten, dead body in a tomb. On the third day, the women went to the tomb and found Jesus missing. An angel asked them, "Why do you seek the living among the dead?" Accounts indicate that the disciples ran to the tomb to look for Jesus. Ponder this: they ran to the ONLY place Jesus promised He would not be. The angel's question is hard, "Why do I seek the living among the dead?" The fear-filled disciples huddled together and waited—I know I've huddled, filled with fear, during some seasons in my life.

Jesus appeared to them, having passed through a locked door! No small talk occurred during this confusing season. Jesus spoke peace. He breathed on them His Holy Spirit. Jesus, then, declared, "'Peace be with you. As the Father has sent me, even so I am sending you.' And when he had said this, he breathed on them and said to them, 'Receive the Holy Spirit'" (John 20:21-22). The breath of our risen Lord breathes peace and life on us and breathes His Spirit into us during every season.

All these things happened quickly, but I imagine it seemed like an eternity to those living the season! They might have felt He left them when he ascended into heaven. Despite all outward appearances, Jesus did not leave them. He was with them and in them through His Spirit.

He promised another manifestation of His Spirit. "These things I have spoken to you while I am still with you. But the

Helper, the Holy Spirit, whom the Father will send in my name, he will teach you all things and bring to your remembrance all that I have said to you" (John 14:25-26).

Worshiping the seasons of life creates stumbling blocks in our faith journey. Perhaps the disciples worshiped the peace-filled seasons, longing for long vineyard walks while Jesus taught them the intricacies of vines and branches. Perhaps we worship the season when our children were little. Maybe we worship some season we've made up for our ideal future. Living in or longing for past seasons steals the joy of the present season; fixating on future seasons steals the joy of the current season!

Jesus' promise, coupled with, "I am the vine; you are the branches. Abide in me" propel us forward in hope through every season! Be present. Feel the word breathing on us, the breath of life. Jesus, the word of God, connects us to Him and Him to us through the word He speaks. We, branches of the one true vine, need to believe and see the connectedness we share with Christ and one another with our hearts.

Jesus' life, the body of the one true vine, is our secure, quiet, abiding place. His profound call to rest in His life and His work touches the deepest need of our complex being. From our connection with Jesus, in this season, we grow and bear mature fruit of abiding as a branch to the vine.

> *We, branches of the one true vine, have connection in every season.*

STUDY 2: ABIDE IN THE VINE

One winter's day in 1998, I saw a team of grafters grafting tiny buds into rootstock in my field. Those people and the images catapulted me into profound discoveries that continue to unfold! The grafting took place in my vineyard, where generations of family members worked the ground and tended the grapes. That day started before sunup in my kitchen, filling my stomach with a big breakfast and filling my heart full of the Scriptures. My body digested food; my heart and mind digested God's word.

Layered with long johns, jeans, coveralls, a thick jacket, hat, and gloves, I walked robotically to my tractor just as the sun rose. I checked the tires and the oil of my trusty steed and put earplugs in. Goggles on. Check, and ready to go. Even today, as I write in the quiet of my home, I can hear the exact noise of the engine firing up. My John Deere tractor pulled a disc to till the damp winter soils of Steinbeck Vineyards.

Dad provided work instructions the day before, so I headed to block 14. Ten-hour days bouncing over the quarter-mile-long rows, back and forth, back and forth, provided hours of prayer time and allowed me to be a student of God's word. That day and every day, I gazed at the tens of thousands of vines around me and prayed. "Jesus, why did you say, 'I am the vine, you are the branches?' Teach me, open my eyes, open my heart, please." On this day, I witnessed a visual of what it means to abide in Christ. This day was the day God gave me this grand gift I now share with you.

With my very own eyes, I witnessed the grafting process!

Ordinarily, we planted one-year-old vines, delivered to us from the nursery, already grafted. I had often observed the tiny, vulnerable branch growing out of the grafted vine. I knew we grafted onto a hardy root known as rootstock to protect our vineyards from disease and the high heat in Paso Robles. This day and this field were different — today was the day I would see, vividly and clearly, the rich meaning of Jesus' call to "abide in me."

Carloads of workers parked single-file on the side of the field adjacent to block 14. They formed teams of three people per row. The first worker held a knife in hand; the worker next picked up a bundle of grape sticks, each about 18" long — I later learned we had provided those cabernet cuttings from an adjacent field. Worker number two also held a sharp knife. The third worker held a roll of stretchy white "tape."

Curiosity got the best of me, so I turned the engine of my tractor off and stood silently, intently watching. Questions rolled around in my mind. I am not fluent in Spanish, so I remained quiet and watched.

One-year-old vines grew in this block. Unlike vines trained on a trellis system, these vines grew like short bushes or shrubs. They were non-fruit-bearing plants known as rootstock. They grow but never produce fruit. I learned that they are resistant to disease and are heat treated at the nursery to resist drought.

The first man bent down near the vine's base and cut a deep slice in its short trunk. The second man that carried the bag of sticks, known as canes, grabbed one, quickly sliced it, and then sliced again. Two cuts. I couldn't figure out what he was doing, so I watched more closely at the next vine. With two swift cuts, he removed a single "bud" from the shoot he was holding. He leaned over, placed that tiny little bud into the precise slice the first man had made, and moved on to the next plant.

The third man wrapped a stretchy tape around the slice and the bud, leaving the tip exposed. The band-aid held the piece in the vine and the bud together, not too tightly. I watched grafting! This team of professional grafters worked at warp speed, so fast my mind and heart couldn't keep up!

My head spun with vineyard questions; my heart raced with Jesus and Scripture questions! I knew I could ask dad about the details of grafting at lunch. My prayer questions began immediately as I got back on my tractor! "Jesus, is the image that I've just witnessed what abiding in you looks like? Am I that little bud, the branch, cut away from the old and placed into your flesh?" "YES," I boldly declared on that day as I resolved to search the Scriptures for more eye-opening, heart-softening images of abiding, healing, and growing!

I watched grafting with my eyes and heart that day many years ago. From that day forward, I've meditated on those images of the flesh-on-flesh relationship of vine and branches. The vine, Jesus, is also the rootstock, the root and descendant of David. We are the little bud, the branch, grafted into Christ, the true vine. The band-aid keeps us bound to Jesus' holy life. We dwell *in* Him.

Question after question rolled off my tongue as I sat with dad at lunch! Dad unfolded the images I saw. The shrub-like vine is a grapevine called the rootstock. Rootstock is a non-fruit-bearing vine that provides a safe home in which the Cabernet thrives for its entire lifespan. Grafting is done to protect the vines from disease, drought, and heat. Grafting takes place once in the life of the vine when they are young. Nurseries usually graft before delivering the vines to us, but they didn't have what we wanted this year, so we planted rootstock, and the team of grafters performed the work in our vineyard.

Grafting

I roll our Jeep to a stop at a vine so I can demonstrate grafting. This 18-inch shoot and every shoot in the vineyard grows evenly spaced buds. At each leaf, there is a little bud. There are 5 buds on this shoot. With my clippers, I snip a "v" shaped bud away from the shoot. The bean-sized bud is so tiny in the palm of my hand.

When cut the vine bleeds. Sap flows from the bud too. The green color of the living shoot invites awe. All of next year's shoot growth and fruit is wound up tightly inside this tiny bud. If we place a cross-section of this bud under a microscope, we can see what is yet to unfold. A collective gasp is uttered.

I make a matching "v" shaped cut into the side of a thicker stick of grape wood, a likeness of the rootstock. I don't actually have rootstock growing in our vineyard because rootstock is planted in the ground. The residual scar from grafting is about three inches above the soil. From the scar upward is the branch. The vine and the root are from the scar downward into the soil. I return to my task, placing the bud into the cut on the vine, wrapping a band-aid around the two pieces, and joining them.

"We are like this, little bud. All of the fruit we will ever bear is in here," I say as I point to my heart. "We're the branch; Jesus is the vine. We abide, we live—*in* Christ." I state while pointing to where the vine and bud join. Jesus was wounded and bled for us; we bled and died when we were cut away from the old life. The sap flowing from the vine and branch creates a healing bond, the bandaid holding us tightly together. Over time, the bond becomes stronger as the scab becomes a scar.

Our abiding relationship with Jesus is flesh on flesh, wholly in His life, grafted in by God the vinedresser. We sit in our Jeep for a bit as we meditate on this profound image.

After a while, I reflected, "The technical name for this little bud is 'scion.' Scion means descendant, an offshoot, offspring, or a branch. We are offspring of Adam and Eve, transformed into branches, descendants of the living vine when the vinedresser cut us away from the old and grafted us into the very life of His son, the vine."

The scion, grafted into the vine, is the branch. I'd always thought of branches sprawling in every direction attached to bigger branches, not knowing how to distinguish between vine and branches. The bud or scion is the branch grafted into the vine just above the soil. That supple branch is trained as the trunk and then onto the trellis system as cordons.

It is important to note that the workers returned to the field a few months later to cut away the shrub just above the graft union. The little bud and the vine had healed as one. The growing bud was now the branch, grafted into the vine. The branches' home in the vine would continue in that relationship for the plant's life.

Every branch grows out of the base of the grapevine, just three inches above the soil, at the place of the graft union. The wound has healed, but the scar remains. Three hundred thousand grapevines in my vineyard sport a scar. The visible scars remind us that the wound made by grafters healed. The scar never goes away. Sap flows to and through the place at which the scion was grafted into the vine and the root. Healed and strong, branches grow and bear fruit from that abiding place.

At Home

We do not, cannot graft ourselves in—it is not possible. We cannot heal ourselves either! We are heirs, offspring, and children of the living God by God's work. We receive. We abide. We live in safety, holiness, and righteousness—forever in Christ. Peter declared, "He himself bore our sins in his body on the tree, that we might die to sin and live to righteousness. By his wounds you have been healed" (1 Peter 2:24).

The very body of Christ, the vine, is our home. We dwell, abide, and live in Him. Living in Christ takes place now, right here, right now. Present tense abides; past tense healed. Recall Paul's declaration to the people of Athens, "Yet he is actually not far from each one of us, for 'In him we live and move and have our being'; as even some of your own poets have said, 'For we are indeed his offspring'" (Acts 17:27b - 28).

The very body of Christ, the vine, is our home.

We abide at home. From a receiving position, we grow up in faith and love bearing mature fruit, the fruit of connection to the one true vine. Ponder Jesus' call to abide, again, with this "grafted in" perspective. "Abide in me, and I in you. As the branch cannot bear fruit by itself, unless it abides in the vine, neither can you, unless you abide in me" (John 15:4).

John, many years later, interpreted Jesus' words, "Whoever confesses that Jesus is the Son of God, God abides in him, and he in God. So we have come to know and to believe the love that God has for us. God is love, and whoever abides in love abides in God, and God abides in him" (1 John 4:15-16).

Abiding in Christ carries the imagery of eternity—the future and the past. How have we died with Christ? We've been cut away from the old; we died. We've been grafted into Christ's life, work, and resurrection. We've been grafted into Christ's life. Our home is in Christ now and is in Christ for all eternity.

When we breathe our last breath on this earth, we will still live, dwelling in the same life of the risen Christ. Today we live by faith in the Son of God, who loves us and gave Himself for us; then, we will live face to face where faith is no longer necessary. Today we live by faith grafted into Christ; then, we will live in Christ face to face. (See Galatians 2)

And there is so much more! We live in Christ, and Christ lives in us. Here are his words again, "Abide in me, and I in you" (John 15:4a). Christ makes His home in us. We are rooted and grounded in Christ, and Christ dwells in us. God abides in us, and we in God through the blood of Christ. Before His "I am the vine" declaration, Jesus said, "I will not leave you as orphans; I will come to you. Yet a little while and the world will see me no more, but you will see me. Because I live, you also will live. In that day you will know that I am in my Father, and you in me, and I in you" (John 14:18-20).

The living vine draws forth the courage to bear the fruit of living in Him and He in us. Each day we are called to a richer, fuller understanding of the work He has done for us and in us. We hear and digest, and we rest in Him.

A band-aid serves as a bookmark in my Bible as a reminder, every day, that my home is *in* Christ and that by His wounds, I am healed. Faith says, "Amen."

Have you been to my home? Yes, indeed, you have. We share a home *in* Christ. We live life at home, together, *in* Christ. All people of faith, of all nations, tribes, or languages, of all time, share our home, grafted into the life of the one true vine. You and I are one, *in* Him, by the work of the Triune God—the vinedresser, the vine, and the Spirit of the vinedresser and the vine.

> *ALL people of faith, of ALL nations, tribes, or languages, of ALL time, share our home grafted into the life of the one true vine.*

STUDY 3: ROOTED IN CHRIST

On that day, more than twenty years ago, I witnessed a branch being grafted into a vine. That shrub-like vine is called the rootstock. The vine into which the bud or branch was grafted is the rootstock. Once that little branch started to grow, the grafters returned to the field and cut off the shrub's growth just above the graft union. Only the roots, the short trunk, and the little branch remained. Three inches of vine grew above ground; the roots grew down more than eighteen inches on the young plant.

Grapevines do not grow from seeds. If you wanted to grow a Cabernet vine I would give you a cutting, a shoot about 18 inches long. You would plant two buds underground—they would grow roots down. The buds above ground would push shoots that would bear Cabernet fruit. If you planted a grape seed, you'd grow a non-fruit-bearing rootstock.

Rootstock was discovered on the East Coast in the late 19th century when careful observers noticed that a non-fruit-bearing grape vine withstood harsh weather and didn't disease like the neighboring vine growing on its own root. Scientific studies and careful propagation led to the worldwide practice of grafting varietals such as Cabernet or Chardonnay onto rootstock.

Rootstock is resistant to a pest known as phylloxera. This pesky aphid does not attack rootstock. It attacks "own-rooted" vines, killing them from the root up. We've discussed branches being grafted onto rootstock because of the rootstock's resistance to phylloxera. Vines can grow from cuttings, but that is not our modern practice because of the attacks of this pest.

Rootstock is chosen based on our soil, climate, and rainfall. Our rootstock choice is one of over one hundred choices. In addition to being disease-resistant, it's resistant to drought and salt.

As human beings, we're susceptible to disease and death on our own roots, the roots of Adam. Jesus, the root and our ascended Lord, is resistant to disease and immune to death, temptation, sin, and Satan. He defeated all in His very life and death — for us. We are grafted into His holy life and into His victory!

The apostle John recorded Jesus' words, "I, Jesus, have sent my angel to testify to you about these things for the churches. I am the root and the descendant of David, the bright morning star" (Revelation 22:16). Isaiah prophesied hundreds of years before, "In that day the root of Jesse, who shall stand as a signal for the peoples—of him shall the nations inquire, and his resting place shall be glorious" (Isaiah 11:10). Paul proclaimed Isaiah's words, "The root of Jesse will come, even he who arises to rule the Gentiles; in him will the Gentiles hope" (Romans 15:12).

The rootstock is Jesus, the vine!

We, the branches, abide in the root, grafted into a new home. Jesus is our stability and structure. "He himself bore our sins in his body on the tree, that we might die to sin and live to righteousness. By his wounds you have been healed" (1 Peter 2:24). We receive the living water and nutrition pumped into our being through the root, through His roots.

Recall Paul's powerful, eternal words that quench our God-created thirst and feed our soul, "That you, being rooted and grounded in love, may have strength to comprehend with all the saints what is the breadth and length and height and depth, and to know the love of Christ that surpasses knowledge, that you may be filled with all the fullness of God (Ephesians 3:17b-19). Paul's words draw our hearts and minds toward Christ—our stability and structure, even in a volatile world where we may feel uprooted and without foundation.

Jesus' words, "I am the root and the descendant of David, the bright morning star," draw our attention upward. He is the root stretching downward toward the earth's core and upward as the Morning Star in the heavens. "Scientists know as little about beneath the land as they know about the heavens," I mutter to the group sitting quietly in my Jeep. Might Jesus have pointed heavenward and declared, "I am the morning star" as he walked with His disciples at the dawn of a new day?

> For when he received honor and glory from God the Father, and the voice was borne to him by the Majestic Glory, "This is my beloved Son, with whom I am well pleased," we ourselves heard this very voice borne from heaven, for we were with him on the holy mountain. And we have the prophetic word more fully confirmed, to which you will do well to pay attention as to a lamp shining in a dark place, until the day dawns and the morning star rises in your hearts. 2 Peter 1:17-21

Light does not exist below the land's surface—roots don't need light. The root, Jesus, doesn't need light—He is the light of the world. Branches need light, so we trust that the root is the light, the morning star, dawning in our hearts. "Your word is a lamp to my feet and a light to my path" (Psalm 119:105). Paul made this connection: "For God, who said, 'Let light shine out of darkness,' has shone in our hearts to give the light of the knowledge of the glory of God in the face of Jesus Christ" (2 Corinthians 4:6).

Solomon's words of wisdom point to Jesus, the root. "No one is established by wickedness, but the root of the righteous will never be moved" (Proverbs 12:3). "Whoever is wicked covets the spoil of evildoers, but the root of the righteous bears fruit" (Proverbs 12:12). Jesus is our righteous root in whom we abide.

My Roots

Our Jeep tour passes my home, a rambling ranch house built in 1921 by Frank and Rosie. Over the past 100 years, six generations have called this "home." My grandmother moved into this home in 1921 when she was just 11 years old. My grandma Hazel raised my Dad and his three siblings in this home. Dad remembers his great grandmother, Barbara Amelia, living here with her son and daughter-in-law during her final years. Mom and Dad called this house "home" for 40 years until 1999 when they completed their dream hilltop home. I was raised here, and I raised my children here. My roots run deep!

Oh, if the walls could talk! We'd hear the noise of pranksters pranking, children chasing, music making, and smell bread baking. Hard-working farmers, farming in California, first by horse and mule, transitioned to tractors in the mid-1930s. They woke before sunrise. Grandma Rosie cooked a big breakfast, and grandpa Frank geared up the team of horses for the day's work.

The old wood stove and fireplace were replaced by a ceramic top stove and forced air heating.

An architectural transition took place with the building of this historic house. The family built the first single-story ranch house in the area. Until that year, homes were built with a basement, ground floor, and upstairs. Tornadoes were prevalent in Geneseo, IL, so shelter was necessary. They learned that there were no tornados in Paso Robles, CA, so there was no need for a basement.

Cold Illinois winters necessitated a sleeping area above the main living floor. The heat created by burning wood in the fireplace on the main level rose throughout the day to warm the sleeping area. Paso gets cold overnight, but not mid-west cold. Freezing winter nights often warm to 50 degrees during sunny days. Most winter storms drop rain, not snow, because of our proximity to California's Central Coast.

Modern insulation didn't exist in 1921. Mom and Dad, tired of drafty walls, hired a contractor to drill holes between every stud and blow insulation into the space. Rather than repair the tongue and groove siding, they chose to stucco the outside of the house. Over the years, each of the three-pillared porches was converted into a living space, giving my home a modern look.

Our Jeep rambles past my play yard. I highlight my swing set, created from an old a-frame auto engine lift. We chuckle at the old being repurposed as we pass our shiny new processing facility with solar panels on the south-facing rooftop.

We chat about the historical significance of our old Syrah vines as we slowly motor by in our Jeep. This old block has yielded prime fruit for 30 years. We're coaxing these old vines along, hoping for many more great seasons while knowing that vines don't produce forever. Wine pioneer Gary Eberle introduced Syrah to California in the 1970s. To this day, the Estrella clone is the most widely grown in our state.

I roll the Jeep down a gentle slope toward the dry creek bed that, during winter rains, becomes a veritable playground for me and my grandchildren. We build dams, throw rocks in the slow-moving water, and splash until we're soaking wet. We walk in the safe places, sinking in the soft sand just a little, pretending to get our boots stuck. Years before, their teenage daddy was forced to leave a boot stuck in the soggy silt because the suction was so great he couldn't get it out.

Our laughter subsides as I point out the many layers of soil revealed in the wall of the twenty-foot-high cliff bank lining the north side of the creek. This cliff bank allows us to see the layers of the soil of Steinbeck Vineyards. The top 8 - 10 inches is our topsoil, the next layer is known as alluvium, and then there is the subsoil. The majority of the roots of grapevines can be found in the top three feet of soil, and the deeper roots go down ten feet or more.

Three hundred thousand vines rooted ten feet deep in the soil beneath the tires of our old Jeep. Above the ground, we see vines and branches, leaves, and buds. We've just seen below the ground. Our thoughts and imagination are drawn deeply downward into the soil and roots. Roots making their way through the topsoil are easy to picture. We visualize how they push deeply downward toward nutrients and water through the harsh subsoil, challenging the most imaginative among us.

Our Roots

Pondering our familial roots, our heritage, in light of Jesus, the root, exercises our faith muscles! Looking at our roots courageously and truthfully will grow mature, balanced fruit. As individuals and members of the body of Christ, we will grow up in love clinging to the stability, structure, nutrients, and water gifted to us by the eternal root.

Journeying into health and healing involves looking back. That look back includes wrestling with how our home of origin affects our actions and thinking. We look back in order to move forward. However, only looking to our parents or grandparents hinders healing. We must trace our roots to our original parents, Adam and Eve. We inherited sin, pain, suffering, and death through their roots. "Therefore, just as sin came into the world through one man, and death through sin, and so death spread to all men because all sinned" (Romans 5:12).

How has, and how does, carrying on the roots of Adam and Eve affect our lives? Our hearts pound within us at God's call to look at our roots. Fear. Yes! Courage. Absolutely! What is God's pure and holy desire? He desires access to every aspect of our roots so the healing sap can lubricate and cleanse every wound. He shines His light, the light of the world, into those beneath the surface areas of our lives to uncover the roots that are ours by being related to Adam and Eve. Here are a few examples of our roots, the roots of Adam and Eve.

Adam and Eve listened to the voice of the evil one. They chose to disobey God's call to obey and worship Him alone. They broke God's only command, "And the Lord God commanded the man, saying, "You may surely eat of every tree of the garden, but of the tree of the knowledge of good and evil you shall not eat, for in the day that you eat of it you shall surely die" (Genesis 2:16-17).

God gave Adam and Eve every tree in the garden He planted for them, but for one. Rather than choose from the many, they ate from the one. Doing "God's only don't" led to hiding, lying, blaming, shame, and a plethora of other profound challenges like pain in childbirth, weeds in fields, dying, and death. We sport these roots!

God creatively designed Adam with a deep longing for healthy roots. God's breath and promise of the root breathed life into Adam. God breathes life into our thirsty souls. Digging deeply and looking at our roots doesn't mean we'll stay there, wallowing in the mire. No!

Shining the light of Christ on our roots oxygenates and breathes life into stale places of our hearts, souls, spirits, emotions, and bodies. We want health — God designed us with that desire. We want to live life fully alive. Knowing and trusting that God rooted and grounded us in Christ ushers us forward in courage and strength as we take a look at our roots.

We want health — God designed us with that desire.

We were born of the same original parents, so despite different stories, we share common roots. The list above, taken from the account of Adam and Eve hiding from God, bears repeating: they felt shame, so they hid, lied, and blamed.

Then the eyes of both were opened, and they knew that they were naked. And they sewed fig leaves together and made themselves loincloths. And they heard the sound of the Lord God walking in the garden in the cool of the day, and the man and his wife hid themselves from the presence of the Lord God among the trees of the garden. But the Lord God called to the man and said to him, "Where are you?" And he said, "I heard the sound of you in the garden, and I was afraid, because I was naked, and I hid myself." He said, "Who told you that you were naked? Have you eaten of the tree of which I commanded you not to eat?" The man said, "The woman whom you gave to be with me, she gave me fruit of the tree, and I ate." Then the Lord God said to the woman, "What is this that you have done?" The woman said, "The serpent deceived me, and I ate." Genesis 3:7-13

Adam and Eve's punishment included death. "By the sweat of your face you shall eat bread, till you return to the ground, for out of it you were taken for you are dust, and to dust you shall return" (Genesis 3:19). God did not create Adam and Eve to know dying and death; God did not create us to know dying and death.

In addition to shame, hiding, and lying, a few deeply ingrained beliefs stemming from my roots include. "Anger is wrong. Emotions, other than joy, are wrong." "If we don't discuss hard topics, they will disappear." "You are a sinner, Jesus died for you, and when you die, you're going to go to heaven." Join me as I unfold these statements and their impact on me.

Anger is wrong. I felt anger. I believed I was wrong for feeling a feeling that I'd been taught was wrong. I lived in shame for feeling anger, and I buried my anger deep in my soul. I couldn't feel joy because I suppressed my anger. Marrying a man who knew how to express anger seemed especially attractive, so I did. Anger is not "wrong," I learned after many years of living in an unsafe home. Rage, an unhealthy expression of a God-given emotion, is wrong. Hurtful. Damaging. Rage breeds death. Death of soul and spirit, death of our marriage followed.

If we don't talk about complex topics, they will go away. I craved conversations of the heart. I wanted to understand all of my "why" questions. Until I didn't. Buried deep in my being, my desire and questions faded into the dark. Sexuality and sex? I read magazines and dated. Relationships? I watched TV and closely watched those around us either staying married or divorcing. Emotional or physical pain? I "lived" as though I were on the outside looking in.

You are a sinner; Jesus died for you, and you will go to heaven when you die. While entirely true, these concepts are hard to comprehend and process without profound conversations of the heart. I wanted to know how to live everyday life in peace and calm! Sinner, yes, of course, I knew that to be true. What about those painful times when someone sinned against me and caused trauma or profound harm? I received their stuff into my being as though I were at fault. They blamed me for their sin. I took it. Shame and confusion reigned at my very core. I buried that too.

We need light, Jesus' light, shining in our dark places to unearth the root of the pain and suffering we may have buried deeply. We need the light, Jesus, shining into the dark places of our hearts and minds. The invitation to grasp the beautiful baptismal imagery — Jesus is our root, now, in the present. Christ, the root, is our foundation, the source of stability, structure, nutrients, and water. We may be tempted to pass quickly through our painful roots, but let's go one step further and explore the root of evil as exposed in Scripture.

Root of Evil

Satan is the root of all evil, period. He wants us and all of Jesus' followers to be broken, living in shame, blame, and lies. He wants us dead, even while we're walking on this earth. Shame, hiding, and lying fulfill his purpose perfectly because they kill the soul and spirit. Keeping us living in fear, paralyzed at the thought of our roots, including dying and death, works well for him. Faith and trusting God, walking in light and life, confessing our sin and receiving mercy, guarding our hearts, and growing in love are wholly abhorred by the evil one.

Satan's work tempts us to live outside our callings. Adam and Eve provide great examples. God had given them essential work — name animals, tend the garden, cling to one another, be fruitful, and multiply. In addition, they had full access to Him, walking and talking in His creative masterpiece. Their relationship with the creator and His creation, their relationship with one another, were the pillars of life. These connections most certainly would have kept them very, very busy. God's desire was for them to live in rest, peace, and joy in the safety of the garden.

Satan's sly deception led to the belief that they didn't have enough. He convinced them not only that they needed to be like God, but they needed to be God. Falling to temptation and sin took them outside of their calling. Disobeying God's call to worship Him through obedience led to shame. Covering their nakedness before each other led to the false belief that they could hide from God.

Hiding, lying, and blaming are deeply rooted in the brokenness of our first parents, as are dying and death. Our creator did not wire us with the skills and ability to uproot shame and fear. Additionally, we were not created nor internally equipped to face dying and death. Abiding and connecting on the most intimate level are foreign to us. Thanks to our original roots, our default is silence, shame, and hiding.

Our world's wickedness flows from the root of Adam and Eve. Murdering babies and the elderly, killing innocent men, women, and children around the globe, greed, mistreating people in the name of god, wars, and starving innocent people are a few examples of wickedness. The damage the root of evil creates is beyond comprehension. Satan wants victory.

Christ won! While we may not see wickedness defeated, Christ won. Solomon, the wisest of all, declared, "The wicked will be cut off from the land, and the treacherous will be rooted out of it" (Proverbs 2:22). We're called to cling to God's word, trusting that He will fulfill His promise of peace and rest, in His way, in His time.

The roots of the new Adam, Jesus, are perfect, holy, righteous, and eternal. We abide in the root, in the life of the vine. "Therefore, as one trespass led to condemnation for all men, so one act of righteousness leads to justification and life for all men. For as by the one man's disobedience the many were made sinners, so by the one man's obedience the many will be made righteous" (Romans 5:18-19).

*The roots of the new Adam are perfect,
holy, righteous, and eternal.*

We abide. God provided an abiding place, the vine, and the root. Our new root is the source of living water, nutrition, stability, and structure. Our new root breeds hope and light. The root in which we abide is perfect, eternal, and not susceptible to sin, Satan, or death.

New Roots; New Life

The Apostle Paul, knowing that our new root and holiness flow from God's action, declared, "If the root is holy, so are the branches" (Romans 11:16b). Paul unfolds this grafting image, "But if some of the branches were broken off, and you, although a wild olive shoot, were grafted in among the others and now share in the nourishing root of the olive tree, do not be arrogant toward the branches. If you are, remember it is not you who support the root, but the root that supports you" (Romans 11:17-18). We don't support the root. We are grafted *into* the root—He supports us.

One of Paul's sermons in Athens included this statement of faith, "For 'in him we live and move and have our being'; as even some of your own poets have said, 'For we are indeed his offspring'" (Acts 17:28). Pause to ponder Paul's profound wisdom and understanding, "Therefore, as you received Christ Jesus the Lord, so walk in him, rooted and built up in him and established in the faith, just as you were taught, abounding in thanksgiving" (Colossians 2:6-7).

The root provides a new home, new life

Jesus prayed these weighty words just before his agonizing journey to the cross,

> For I have given them the words that you gave me, and they have received them and have come to know in truth that I came from you; and they have believed that you sent me. I am no longer in the world, but they are in the world, and I am coming to you. Holy Father, keep them in your name, which you have given me, that they may be one, even as we are one. I do not ask that you take them out of the world, but that you keep them from the evil one. John 17:8, 11, 15

We are one in Christ, one with one another, fellow branches grafted into the vine and root. As branches abiding in the vine and root, we are kept by the holy one who defeated evil for all time. He calls us to action. We are called to fight evil and corruption from this rooted, safe position in Christ. Paul lays at our feet this familiar image,

> Finally, be strong in the Lord and in the strength of his might. Put on the whole armor of God, that you may be able to stand against the schemes of the devil. For we do not wrestle against flesh and blood, but against the rulers, against the authorities, against the cosmic powers over this present darkness, against the spiritual forces of evil in the heavenly places. Therefore take up the whole armor of God, that you may be able to withstand in the

evil day, and having done all, to stand firm. Stand therefore, having fastened on the belt of truth, and having put on the breastplate of righteousness, and, as shoes for your feet, having put on the readiness given by the gospel of peace. In all circumstances take up the shield of faith, with which you can extinguish all the flaming darts of the evil one; and take the helmet of salvation, and the sword of the Spirit, which is the word of God. Ephesians 6:10-17

Be strong in the Lord and in the strength of his might are abiding words. Nutrients and water flow from the land into the root, through the root and vine to the branches. In and through describes the flow of life and energy in our lives. We abide in Christ the vine and the root; through Him flow nutrients, water, stability, and structure. Christ, the root, is our foundation and source of life.

STUDY 4: THE SAP—THE LIFEBLOOD

Our late afternoon Jeep tour leads us past a recently pruned block of Merlot. As we're bouncing around discussing pruning, I catch a glimpse of a tiny drip of sap glistening in the waning sun. As we looked closely, we see that the pruning wounds on every shoot were bleeding.

Grapevines bleed! Drip after drip slowly pours out of the cut right before our eyes. A scab will form, and the lifeblood of the vine, the sap, will flow only on the inside of the vine.

Sap flows throughout the vine and branches carrying nutrients and water to every cell. Complex and intricately woven as the DNA of the vine and branches, the sap carries the code throughout every cell. Every single grapevine, regardless of varietal differences, contains life-giving sap.

The image of the sap flowing at all times dwelled powerfully in my heart. I captured a photo of three tiny drips of sap flowing from a fresh wound and placed it on my screen saver. This image kept me alive and focused on God's healing work during dark, traumatic days. Being surrounded by healing grapevines gave me hope that Christ's lifeblood flowing in me would also bring healing.

Years later, I received an unexpected phone call—on Good Friday. "You offer Jesus tours? We want one today. We'll be to Steinbeck by noon!" I fired up my Willys Jeep and greeted two enthusiastic couples. After briefly introducing our family's rich heritage, we boarded the Jeep. They chuckled about the Jeep tour being short because, only 50 yards into the tour, I nosed into a row of unpruned Chardonnay vines and turned off our tour vehicle.

We usually prune Chardonnay in early January. This year was different. These 35-year-old vines had lived their life span, and the time had come to replace them. Un-pruned and untrained, the unruly shoots were a mess. I wasn't shy about cutting into an unwieldy shoot.

We sat silently in utter amazement as we watched sap pour forth from the wound on Good Friday. Drip after drip, the cells released sap right before our eyes. We cried. We worshiped. We celebrated. Each meditated on Christ, the true vine's lifeblood pouring out. I can't tell you how long we sat at that bleeding vine, but I can tell you that our hearts were filled with the splendid visuals we had witnessed.

The Sap and The Blood

Blood flows throughout our complex bodies at all times, carrying oxygen, nutrients, and water to every cell. Additionally, our blood carries toxins into the organs God designed to cleanse our blood. Complex and intricately woven as the DNA of our body, our blood carries our unique code. Every person is unique; every person has much in common through the blood in our bodies.

Blood, like sap flowing to every cell of every branch, carries nutrients and water to every cell in the human body. From the tips of our fingers to the ends of our toes, blood pumps through our heart to those outermost cells held in place by our largest organ, our skin. Our organs play in concert, a grand concerto composed by God. We echo with David, "I praise you, for I am fearfully and wonderfully made. Wonderful are your works; my soul knows it very well" (Psalm 139:14).

The life we have in common, with all people everywhere, is our blood. Our features and skin color may differ, but our blood is red and comprises white blood cells, red blood cells, and platelets. And, by God's design, we are unique individuals, as our fingerprints and DNA prove. The life we share with Christians everywhere is our blood and the blood of Christ in us. We are grafted into His holy life, and His blood and our blood flow together.

The Cabernet Sauvignon bud, grafted into the rootstock, doesn't lose its unique DNA but becomes more fully what it is meant to be. Disease free and protected from drought and heat. We, the branches, grafted into the vine, the rootstock, don't lose our individuality. We become more fully who we're meant to be. We abide in the healthy, holy root.

Jesus is resistant to sin, death, and Satan; He is resistant to the disease Adam shared with us. Grafted into His life, we inherit those gifts while maintaining our uniqueness.

When wounded by a sharp object, our skin opens up, and blood flows out. The outward flow of blood cleanses and keeps harmful germs out. Similar to the healing properties of the sap of a vine, white blood cells and platelets rush to the wound to begin the healing process. First, blood coagulates and then forms a protective cover known as a scab. Eventually, the scab falls off, and the visible sign of the wound is a scar.

Scars on the vine branches remind us of the wounds and healing that have taken place over the years. Counting back every year of the life of a vine, through the scars on an old vine, gives us pause to rejoice at how many times the branches of the vine have been wounded and have healed. Scars on our bodies remind us of wounds we've endured.

Wounds of the heart, soul, spirit, and mind require blood flow to heal too. Christ's blood powerfully pumps to all areas of our being. Christ's blood cleanses every nook and cranny, even in unknown areas. Christ's blood is life. Our wounded being needs rich nutrition; Jesus is the bread of life. Unhealed wounds need refreshing water; Jesus is the living water.

This rich imagery can be taken further as we open our hearts and minds to Christ's declaration of the relationship of the vine to branches. Think of the many leaves, even on a single shoot. Leaves take in light and convert it to energy. Shoots do not heal or grow in darkness.

Jesus is the light. Light equals energy. Christ's blood carries oxygen. We need oxygen! Jesus is the breath of the living God. Jesus heals—through His blood.

As our Jeep passes block 5, this story came to me. Dad came to me one day and said, "You have to get a picture of this! Look at this, right at the top of the trunk. This part of the branch is not growing." Dad noticed that one branch on one particular vine was not growing or producing quality fruit. It was stunted. Water was getting to the vine, so that wasn't the cause of the atrophy. Upon close examination, Dad found a tendril wound tightly around the shoot.

Tendrils are flexible, spring-like mechanisms growing in many places on young shoots of a vine. They wrap around trellis wire or post to give the branches structure and stability.

The tendril allows the shoots to move in the wind, but not so much that they snap or break. Tendrils help bear the weight of the fruit as well. As the season progresses and the weight of the fruit increases, tendrils harden to provide the necessary support.

Likely years earlier, a tendril had wrapped around this young branch. The woody tendril did not get cut away, year after year, during winter pruning because it was virtually invisible to the eye. As the branch grew in girth over the next few years, the hardened tendril did not give way. The tendril cut off sap flow. Girdled and strangled, cut off from nutrients and water, the branch atrophied.

The tendril grown from the branch of that vine cut off the necessary flow of the life-giving sap. Growth, healing, and fruit were impossible because sap could not freely flow to every cell beyond the tightly wound tendril.

The branch strangled itself, cutting off the all-important sap flow to every cell. Every cell of our being, heart, mind, spirit, and soul needs Christ's healing blood to flow unrestricted. We, like the tendril, can strangle ourselves by not allowing access to certain areas of our being, deep parts of us that need healing blood flow.

Every cell of our being, our heart, mind, spirit, and soul need Christ's healing blood to flow unrestricted

Fear, shame, and denial strangled me. Untrained in matters of the heart and with nowhere to turn for safe conversation, I buried essential aspects of my being behind a fast-paced work life. I was afraid that if you knew me, you wouldn't, or couldn't, possibly love me. More than that, I was confused at my volatile internal world—shame for just being alive paralyzed my heart and spirit. Denial of emotional and spiritual pain gripped my soul. Chipper and strong on the outside, I cut off cleansing blood flow on the inside.

The image of the tendril strangling the shoot by not allowing the sap to flow to the cells stirred my heart. The journey of the soul and spirit summarizes the scary, beautifully profound path God called me into. Grafted safely into the life of Christ and over a period of many years, lifeblood flowed to all aspects of my being. Surrounded by growth and change, I embraced and mirrored the images of the vine.

Watching sap drip out of a wounded shoot and the word of God calling me to live brought slow and steady healing. Fear gave way to courage; shame melted away in mercy; truth replaced denial. I begged the vinedresser, the vine, and the Spirit of the living God to remove any obstacle restricting blood flow to every cell in my being.

There's more to the story of that strangled shoot. Dad took action! I watched my father take a sharp saw and severe the atrophied shoot at the strangling point. A young shoot grew up from the healthy branch, and within a year, the new shoot was thriving and bearing prime fruit. The whole branch didn't need removal from the vine; the shoot required deep wounding to restore the entire branch to health.

We know how to live wounded. We know how to cut God off from shameful parts of our being. We want to know how to live healed! Many live robust and chipper outside while feeling strangled and wounded, hurting and lonely inside. We're not alone. We know how to live wounded; we want to live healed!

Our living God calls us to live life fully alive in Him. The vinedresser calls us to live healed in the blood of His Son. Sin is forgiven, and brokenness is healed in Christ. We are free to grow as thriving children of the living God.

Energy

Vines and branches draw energy from the soil by absorbing and carrying nutrients via the sap through every cell. The energy necessary to healthy vines and branches flows into the plant from outside sources. Leaves on shoots take in sunlight. In a complex transfer, the leaves convert that light energy into carbohydrates. The cells feed on the rich nutrients. Branches don't feed themselves.

Additional nutrients are added through our drip irrigation system twice a year. Experts test the soils and the leaves a few times each year, directing our application of just the right amount of nutrients. Too much nitrogen or potassium stunts growth—vines and branches need balance. The vinedresser bases his nutrient application decisions on the advice of experts. He's an expert, and he relies on science to help him.

We, branches, must engage and trust outside sources for our energy needs. We need experts to help us identify proper nutrition and exercise for our bodies. We may need physical therapy and spiritual or psychological care to help us attain balance and flow of energy to all aspects of our being.

Asking Jesus for help takes courage. Receiving support opens up possibilities for new energy and growth. Jesus said I am the light of the world, the light of your world; I am the bread of life, bread for your life.

Scripture provides outside nutrients. God calls us to take the nutrients in His word into our being, chew on, and digest this food for energy. The word of God creates and sustains, it wounds and heals. God's word not only reveals Jesus—the word is Jesus. He took on human skin, flesh, and blood. Jesus is life and light and energy for us and in us. As we receive and grow, the word of Jesus works through us.

Jesus' best friend recorded these words many years after Jesus' death, resurrection, and ascension:

> In the beginning was the Word, and the Word was with God, and the Word was God. He was in the beginning with God. All things were made through him, and without him was not any thing made that was made. In him was life, and the life was the light of men." John continued, "And the Word became flesh and dwelt among us, and we have seen his glory, glory as of the only Son from the Father, full of grace and truth." John 1:1-4, 14

Saul spent his energy murdering followers of Jesus. Blinded by the light and healed by the word, Saul turned from his former ways and was renamed, Paul. He directed all of his energy into the proclamation of Jesus, the living God, who brought him out of darkness into light. Paul's words in Colossians help us understand that he was not working under his energy. "For this I toil, struggling with all his energy that he powerfully works within me" (Colossians 1:29).

We, too, are called by the vinedresser and the vine into a deep understanding that our energy is not the trustworthy source of strength and healing. We must rely on an energy source outside ourselves.

The lifeblood of Christ, the energy of Christ, flows to every cell of our being. We don't heal our wounds. Jesus heals them. We don't cause spiritual growth, the energy of Christ brings growth. Healed and growing, we produce the fruit in keeping with abiding. We trust, receive, and give. We reflect the light and energy of God working in us.

Paul begs us to grasp hold, with our heart and whole being these powerful, energy-filled words: "the same power of God that raised Jesus from the dead works in us" (Ephesians 1:19-21)!

Paul stands before us, calling us to rely not on our energy but on the power God worked to raise Jesus from the grave. God's great might worked in Christ; God's great strength and might are at work in us.

Energy-less? Christ calls us to focus on His energy working in us. Fearful that healing of all aspects of our being isn't possible? Cling to the word and work of God. We're called to rest in the life-breeding light of Christ. The energy of the word of God was manifested in the life of the vine, the root. Jesus calls us to heal and grow in His very life!

STUDY 5: HEALING IN CHRIST

Wounded vines heal. Branches and shoots of vines heal. Different types and depths of healing take place during different seasons in the life of the vine.

Winter healing takes place as pruned vines heal from the severe wound made by the sharp shears of the pruners. Shoots, wounded during spring leaf thinning and summer fruit thinning, heal. Picking the fruit in the fall creates wounds that heal. The deepest of all cuts, the one made on the vine and branch during grafting, heal under the band-aid. The vine and branch grow together as one.

These comforting examples of healing emanate hope! The recovery of the vines and the vine draw our attention away from our wounds to the possibility of the healing of our wounds. We don't ignore wounds, we believe that healing is possible! God created vines and branches to heal; He most certainly created us to heal.

Jump in my Jeep, and I'll tell you a story about an extraordinary healing place in Steinbeck Vineyards—Row 124.

After crossing the dry creek bed and heading up the dirt road, I rolled our Jeep to a stop on a little knoll with a stunning view—a lone oak tree in the distant towers above the old vines. The sandy, rocky soil extends up from the tree-lined dry river bed. The gentle slope provides rich contour to the evenly spaced and perfectly trained vines.

We pause at the little wood sign that reads, "Cast Your Cares On Him. Row 124." A pile of rocks rests below the vines of Row

124. This is a special place for leaving my burdens. Not all of these rocks are mine. Many people have journeyed here, to the foot of the vines, and placed their burdens in Row 124.

On one of our many vineyard walks, a friend shared an observation with me. "You are an excellent teacher, but you don't believe what you are telling the ladies. You say, 'Jesus loves you, but you don't believe that His love is for you.'" I was taken aback!

Right then and there, I had two choices. I could have easily walked away, hurt by her honest observation. Instead, I chose to listen and hear rather than reject her words. However, deep down, I knew she was right. I was passionate about telling you powerful Jesus stories of healing and redemption. Because I lived in fear and shame, Jesus' words spoken passionately from my head knowledge, fell far short of my heart.

My prayers changed that day as I began asking Jesus to allow me to soak in His mercy. As I reflect many years later, I thank God for working through my friend's wake-up call to draw my attention to the possibility of healing.

Another vineyard walk with my friend led us toward the spot of one of my (many) ATV accidents. As I told the story of the injuries at that place, and subsequently holding my pain silently out of embarrassment, she blurted out, "I'm going to walk with you to every place on this vineyard where you've been hurt, and you can tell me all about it." I hung my head and muttered, "there are so many places." "I don't care," she declared firmly. Relief flooded through me—I was no longer alone.

Exasperated at our third stop and story, she blurted out, "this is going to take too long!" On that rainy day in February—my friend suggested a bold move. As I shared my burdens, she discerned that they were too much for me to carry and too much for her too. She said, "let's lay down right here," pointing to a spot between the vine rows. I protested, "it's raining!" Her reply: "so?"

We lay down together, in the mud, in the rain. She begged God to take my heavy load—all of the injuries, all of the wounds, and all of the scars—all of them. We cried. She picked up a rock and held it above us. She said, "Picture your burdens in this rock. We're going to give them all to God." With that, she plunked that rock down under the vines. We knelt in the mud and the rain and prayed, "God, teach us how to cast our cares on you."

Row 124 began the healing process of letting go of trauma and shame. Our Row 124 prayers served as formative moments where God moved my faith from my head to my heart.

Fast forward to a few weeks later. As we walked, I began telling a story of an injury, one of the same burdens I had begged God to take in the form of a big rock I plopped in Row 124. My friend grabbed my hand and said, "We're hiking back to 124, and I'm going to pick up that rock and put it in your hands to carry back here." "NO, NO," I protested! "I want to learn to give it to God."

Healing sap and Row 124—God worked through a friend, the vine, and the vineyard to further the healing process in my heart and life. What rock or boulder would you leave in Row 124? We will pause for as long as it takes to pick a rock, plop it down, and pray for healing.

The powerful symbol of giving burdens to God and walking away trusting God to heal holds rich meaning!

Pain—A Common Denominator

The burdens left in the boulders at the feet of Jesus have a common denominator—pain. All who have journeyed to Row 124 express pain! They write on their rock or talk to me about carrying the heavy load for far too long. They tell me about their pain. Emotional pain. Mental pain. Physical pain. Spiritual pain. I understand.

The death of a spouse or a child, illness or injury, children suffering, trauma, violence, depression, confusion, angry spouse, anger turned inward, rape, sexual assault, addiction, drugs, alcohol, pornography. The list goes on and on and on!

There are those who plop their burden in Row 124 and want to leave all pain associated with their burdens. God created us to feel pain. God's magnificent design of our whole being requires that we feel the pain to heal from pain. "Humble yourselves, therefore, under the mighty hand of God so that at the proper time he may exalt you, casting all your anxieties on him, because he cares for you" (1 Peter 5:6-7). While processing the pain, we heal and grow.

> *God's magnificent design —*
> *feel the pain to heal from pain*

Running from pain creates more pain. Pain teaches us. Pain teaches that we are alive, that we can feel. Pain teaches us to care for our body, heart, soul, spirit, mind, and emotions. Pain teaches us to ask hard questions. Pain teaches us to seek help to answer deep, very important questions.

We have a tremendous opportunity to learn from pain.

We learn that as we leave our burdens, one at a time, at the foot of the vine. God works through brokenness, through our stories, not apart from them. Running from pain wearies our spirit and soul. Leaning into pain allows us to witness God's pain as well as God's ultimate plan for us where there will be no more pain or tears. "For the Lamb amid the throne will be their shepherd, and he will guide them to springs of living water, and God will wipe away every tear from their eyes" (Revelation 7:17).

Pain is a common bond we share with all people everywhere, even though our stories differ. Our desire to run from, rather than feel, pain binds us together too. As we run, we desensitize and dull our pain.

Pain-numbing ways to run from pain abound! Anything we use in excess may be our Novocain. Numbing leads to even more boulders we'll eventually need to plunk down in Row 124!

We need each other, journey partners, to lean in and heal from our wounds. Christ places people in our lives to walk with us into the loving arms of Jesus, the great healer. He leaned into the pain of this world, His pain, death, and the grave for us. Peter declared, "He himself bore our sins in his body on the tree, that we might die to sin and live to righteousness. By his wounds you have been healed" (1 Peter 2:24).

Relief and Healing

God did not introduce pain into His creation. Pain came into this world through Adam and Eve's disobedience. Immediately after they ate the fruit of the tree of knowledge of good and evil, pain appeared. Attempts to run from and numb their pain included hiding, lying, blaming, and shame.

Imagine their pain and grief as God escorted them out of the Garden of Eden. Unlike you and me, they would have been able to recall perfection. Oh, how they must have longed to walk and talk with God again!

The dust outside the garden must have felt strangely familiar to Adam. God had formed his being of the dust. He'd been there before. His lifeless form was created there and, before the breath of God, was mere dust.

God formed Adam out of dust. God raised Adam from that dust through His breath. God intentionally placed Adam in the Garden of Eden. "Then the Lord God formed the man of dust from the ground and breathed into his nostrils the breath of life, and the man became a living creature. And the Lord God planted a garden in Eden, in the east, and there he put the man whom he had formed" (Genesis 2:7-8).

God sent Adam and Eve out of the garden.

> Then the Lord God said, "Behold, the man has become like one of us in knowing good and evil. Now, lest he reach out his hand and take also of the tree of life and eat, and live forever." Therefore the Lord God sent him out from the garden of Eden to work the ground from which he was taken. He drove out the man, and at the east of the garden of Eden he placed the cherubim and a flaming sword that turned every way to guard the way to the tree of life. Genesis 3:22-24

Because they disobeyed God's only command, Adam and Eve would return to dust. Their life changed forever because of their knowledge of good and evil.

While living outside their once-perfect home, they experienced pain. Eve experienced pain in childbirth and Adam as he farmed among thorns and thistles. Adam and Eve experienced the pain of their oldest son killing his brother! When Adam and Eve breathed their last breath on earth, they died. Their bodies returned to dust.

God promised relief and healing. God would send Jesus through Adam and Eve's offspring. The promised one would crush the tempter one day in the future. Through God's promise of healing through their offspring, eternity was reality. Rather than walk side by side with God, they lived by faith in God's promise and presence among them.

From that time forward, each wound and every moment of pain throughout Scripture provided an opportunity to trust God's provision, His total relief, and complete healing. Through God's rich promise of the one to come, Adam and Eve as well as all believers after them entered perfection after their death. God created them for an eternal relationship, but they had to pass through pain and the punishment for sin.

Moses disobeyed God's instructions and received God's punishment. "You will not enter the promised land" (Deuteronomy 34:1-8). Moses trusted God with his life; Moses believed in God's promise of eternal life. When Moses breathed his last breath on this earth he gazed at the promised land from the mountaintop. Where was Moses when he died? The promised land! His punishment, death, brought him face to face with Jesus, minus a million complaining people!

Stephen, Paul, and Peter endured incredible pain, knowing that complete relief and healing would be realized when they breathed their last breath on this earth. Each, in their own way, proclaimed complete healing, in Christ, in the present.

All endure pain, some more than others. God calls us to trust that relief and healing will be complete, not on this earth, but in the eternal home Jesus prepared for us. Yet, at the same time, healing is complete now. Where do we live now? Grafted into and healed in the very flesh of Jesus, the true, eternal vine!

Healing is now; relief and complete healing are not yet. We long, as Paul said, to put on our heavenly dwelling. When we are fully clothed in our heavenly home, we will look back, knowing the pain we endured provided a rich opportunity to witness our faith and hope in Christ.

> For we know that if the tent that is our earthly home is destroyed, we have a building from God, a house not made with hands, eternal in the heavens. For in this tent we groan, longing to put on our heavenly dwelling, if indeed by putting it on we may not be found naked. For while we are still in this tent, we groan, being burdened—not that we would be unclothed, but that we would be further clothed, so that what is mortal may be swallowed up by life. God, who has prepared us for this very thing, has given us the Spirit as a guarantee. 2 Corinthians 5:1-5
>
> I heard a loud voice from the throne saying, "Behold, the

dwelling place of God is with man. He will dwell with them, and they will be his people, and God himself will be with them as their God. He will wipe away every tear from their eyes, and death shall be no more, neither shall there be mourning, nor crying, nor pain anymore, for the former things have passed away." Revelation 21:3-4

Lord, I Believe; Help My Unbelief!

Jesus healed the man at the pool of Bethesda. Scripture tells us that the blind, lame, and paralyzed lay at the edge of this pool. The fastest among the wounded made their way into the water, one person per day, as it was being stirred. Through the water, they were healed. Day after day, a lame man lay waiting for an opportunity to make his way into the water. He'd been disabled for 38 years. He wasn't able to get there himself. He needed help.

Jesus approached and asked the lame man, "Do you want to be healed?" A simple answer, yes, would have served the man well. The man answered, "Sir, I have no one to put me into the pool when the water is stirred up, and while I am going another steps down before me" (John 5:7).

Daily, the man watched people make their way into the pool and rise from the water healed. The healing was for those who were quick to get into the water at the right time, but not for him! Without hesitation or explanation, Jesus said, "Get up, take up your bed, and walk" (John 5:8). The man walked. The word of Jesus healed him.

Jesus, God in skin, was present with that particular man that day and dwelled among the people of that day. He healed. He cleansed. Jesus proclaimed Himself Messiah, Lord of life and Lord over death.

It's hard to imagine or trust that we have more, but the truth is, we have more! How much more do we have? We've been gifted with the Scriptures, the word of God, each word written for our healing. We know the cross and the empty tomb! We have the water and the word in baptism. Old Testament believers looked forward in faith without knowing the whole story.

We live grafted into the life of Jesus, and Jesus dwells in us. Jesus heals us through His very life; Jesus heals us by dwelling in us. Jesus' words are again before us: "Abide in me, and I in you" (John 15:4a). Isaiah foretold of Jesus' dwelling place with us, in us to revive and heal us:

> For thus says the One who is high and lifted up, who inhabits eternity, whose name is Holy: "I dwell in the high and holy place, and also with him who is of a contrite and lowly spirit, to revive the spirit of the lowly, and to revive the heart of the contrite. Isaiah 57:15

> I have seen his ways, but I will heal him; I will lead him and restore comfort to him and his mourners, creating the fruit of the lips. Peace, peace, to the far and to the near, says the Lord, "and I will heal him." Isaiah 57:18-19

Jesus asks today, "Do you want to be healed?" What might our answer be? We could quickly and indeed devise a list of excuses for the impossible thought. A simple yes suffices. Jesus wraps up our limited definition of healing in His loving arms and calls us in close. He says, don't let your fear-filled heart hold you back.

I know your wounds and your pain. Open your eyes, hear with your ears, understand with your heart, turn to me, and I will heal you. Faith declares, yes, Amen!

Faith mirrors the words of the suffering father, too, "I believe; help my unbelief!" Here is the account of the man who asked Jesus for compassion and received much more,

> And they brought the boy to him. And when the spirit saw him [Jesus], immediately it convulsed the boy, and he fell on the ground and rolled about, foaming at the mouth. And Jesus asked his father, "How long has this been happening to him?" And he said, "From childhood. And it has often cast him into fire and into water, to destroy him. But if you can do anything, have compassion on us and help us." And Jesus said to him, "'If you can'! All things are possible for one who believes." Immediately the father of the child cried out and said, "I believe; help my unbelief!" And when Jesus saw that a crowd came running together, he rebuked the unclean spirit, saying to it, "You mute and deaf spirit, I command you, come out of him and never enter him again." And after crying out and convulsing him terribly, it came out, and the boy was like a corpse, so that most of them said, "He is dead." But Jesus took him by the hand and lifted him up, and he arose. Mark 9:20-27

Immediate relief and healing took place for many as Jesus walked this earth 2,000 years ago. The blind received their sight, the lame walked, lepers were cleansed, and the dead were raised. Immediately whole, fully restored people praised Jesus. We may be tempted to say, that was then, this is now, as we long for immediate healing. Jesus can and does heal immediately today. We trust that He works healing in other ways too.

The vines and branches teach us rich lessons about healing. Different wounds take different amounts of time to heal. Deep wounds take the longest to heal; shallow wounds take the least amount of time—the graft wound heals slowly over two years, the pruning wounds take a month to heal fully, and wounds created by thinning take a week to mend.

We want to heal rapidly, smoothly, and in a linear fashion. God chooses to work in a variety of ways, differently for different people. Our journeys drawn on a sheet of paper might look like squiggly, incongruent lines, overlapping circles, spirals, or tornadoes. Not linear in any way, our healing journeys have likely been and continue to be a beautiful mess of God's work. He continues to melt away our fears and doubts, urging us to step into mercy daily, calling us to fix our eyes on Him.

"Lord, we believe; help our unbelief!"

Our often isolated hearts cry out, "we need community in the beautiful mess!" We are not alone! We need one another, a community of weary yet strong, authentic, faith-filled beautiful messes with whom to journey. The God-given ache for connection draws us into a life of feeding our hunger with the bread of life, quenching our thirst with living water and the wine of restoration.

STUDY 6: GROWING IN CHRIST

Grapevines grow. Branches and shoots of vines grow. Watching growth over these past years has given me a deeper understanding of growing in Christ. God created us to grow. Prayerfully, these images and a few examples from my personal growth story will urge you toward continued courage to welcome growth.

My east-facing front window gives me the overwhelming privilege of greeting the rising sun daily. For many years I watched the sun rise over vines planted in 1982. As they aged, the gnarled gray-brown wood of the branches provided the canvas onto which the tiny shoots burst forth. Grapevines have a lifespan and these 35-year-old vines stopped thriving and producing prime fruit. We tore them out and planted new vines grafted at the nursery.

Protective tubes called grow tubes, surround each baby vine planted in my ten-acre block. We place grow tubes around the vines to shelter them from pests and protect them from the elements. When the vines are strong enough to be trained onto the trellis system, around year two, we remove the tubes.

Six thousand baby vines, grow tubes, the trellis system, and drip hose replaced those stately old vines. The baby vines cannot be seen yet, but I will soon look out my window as the sun rises and rejoice as tender shoots peek out the top of the "grow" tubes as they reach for the sunshine.

The vines were growing, I was not. After years of doing the same things that weren't working, I had to admit I was stuck. Love for Jesus and His word was real. Faith was evident in my life. I thought that if I were more, more of something, the volatile raging of my former spouse would stop. "He was nice to others; surely, if I were better, he'd be nice to me," I reasoned.

The possibility of growth glimmered as I slowly healed. Jesus' questions permeated the walls of my broken heart: "What do you want me to do for you?" "Do you want to be healed?"

Courage called. Life called. The dark temptation to box in and limit God's healing faded. My fear of healing and growing began to diminish as I listened to God's call to grow. Staying stuck faded away in the light of these critical growing questions. Oxygen, light, water, and nutrients began to flow through the word of God and the help of experts.

Calling in the Specialists

I've watched my father, the vinedresser, work in my vineyard. His vast knowledge, grounded in years of practical experience, guides their viticulture decisions. And he never hesitate to call in specialists when concerns arise beyond their scope of expertise. When vines that should be growing stall, vinedressers call in experts.

My son did the same when his newborn baby didn't grow. Their three-month-old wasn't growing. She had only gained a few ounces from birth. They sought out expert doctors. The very best specialists concluded, "She's healthy and tiny!"

The need to call in specialists when vines and babies don't grow seems to be common sense. I needed to courageously mirror that practice when my heart and soul growth stalled. The vineyard and my children provided rich examples for me.

Are we growing? Do we need specialists?

Specialists can be scary because they might tell us something we don't know! They might ask hard questions, recommend that we make changes to our practices, or introduce necessary elements to stimulate growth.

The first and primary specialist is Jesus, the vine. Jesus calls us to look to His word in new and different ways. He calls us to rest our hearts in the facts of the work He accomplished. He calls us into the stories as though they are our stories. Jesus calls us to receive His questions. Here are a few to ponder: "What do you want me to do for you?" (Matthew 20:32, Mark 10:36, March10:51, Luke 18:41) "Do you understand what I have done to you?" (John 13:12) He also calls us to imagine walking those dusty streets with Him.

He calls us to look closely at His "I am" statements and trust that He is the great "I am" for us.

Jesus, the divine specialist, doesn't recommend introducing oxygen, light, water, and food into branches from a distance. Jesus is the resurrection and life; Jesus is light; Jesus is living water; Jesus is the bread of life. His words are truth and life.

All other relationships we seek to help us grow must flow from the primary specialist. Experts may include pastors, teachers, therapists, small groups, and friends. In loving wisdom, they challenge us to think about those things we don't yet know, ask hard questions, recommend changes, and introduce elements to stimulate growth.

We may feel naked before Jesus, the divine specialist, as he sees through our outer facade. We feel vulnerable. Visualize that little grow tube He places around us to protect us as we develop those tender, vulnerable shoots. His word guards our hearts and spirit, protecting us as we grow.

Jesus knows the truth of our brokenness, and He loves us with everlasting love. His love conquered the cross and grave for us. His righteousness covers us. Growing flows from our intimate relationship with Him, in Him.

Growing Words from Wise Branches

Growing words flowed from the lips and pen of a notable branch of the one true vine, the apostle Paul. Paul, formerly Saul, worked with all his might to kill growth. Like the Jews before him, Paul wanted all who followed Christ dead. Paul's conversion (Acts 9) took place through the words spoken by Stephen, through blinding light, and through nutritious words delivered by Ananias.

Paul's new faith grew rapidly and freely. His faith matured exponentially without any hard work on his part! His faith developed because branches grafted into Christ's life grow! Paul's deepest desire, after his initial growth, was that branches of the one true vine grow. Paul's bold proclamation, brought forth through the power and energy of Christ at work in him, urges us today into deeper faith, hope, and love.

> We ought always to give thanks to God for you, brothers, as is right, because your faith is growing abundantly, and the love of every one of you for one another is increasing.
> 2 Thessalonians 1:3

> Having the eyes of your hearts enlightened, that you may know what is the hope to which he has called you, what

are the riches of his glorious inheritance in the saints, and what is the immeasurable greatness of his power toward us who believe, according to the working of his great might that he worked in Christ when he raised him from the dead and seated him at his right hand in the heavenly places, far above all rule and authority and power and dominion, and above every name that is named, not only in this age but also in the one to come. And he put all things under his feet and gave him as head over all things to the church, which is his body, the fullness of him who fills all in all. Ephesians 1:18-23

For it is all for your sake, so that as grace extends to more and more people it may increase thanksgiving, to the glory of God. So we do not lose heart. Though our outer self is wasting away, our inner self is being renewed day by day. For this light momentary affliction is preparing for us an eternal weight of glory beyond all comparison, as we look not to the things that are seen but to the things that are unseen. For the things that are seen are transient, but the things that are unseen are eternal. 2 Corinthians 4:16-18

Speaking the truth in love, we are to grow up in every way into him who is the head, into Christ, from whom the whole body, joined and held together by every joint with which it is equipped, when each part is working properly, makes the body grow so that it builds itself up in love. Ephesians 4:15-16

To them God chose to make known how great among the Gentiles are the riches of the glory of this mystery, which is Christ in you, the hope of glory. Him we proclaim, warning everyone and teaching everyone with all wisdom, that we may present everyone mature in Christ. For this I toil, struggling with all his energy that he powerfully works within me. Colossians 1:27-29

Growing in Maturity

Paul's words must be understood and cherished from deep within Paul's story. Saul's name changed; Saul's heart changed. His rapid growth in Christ flowed from stoning Stephen to a horrible death—with rocks! Saul heard Stephen's message, and he gnashed his teeth at Stephen. (Acts 7:54) The ESV translated Acts 8:1, "Saul approved of Stephen's execution." NASB reads, "Saul was in hearty agreement with putting him to death." Here is the account.

> And as they were stoning Stephen, he called out, "Lord Jesus, receive my spirit." And falling to his knees he cried out with a loud voice, "Lord, do not hold this sin against them." And when he had said this, he fell asleep. And Saul approved of his execution. And there arose on that day a great persecution against the church in Jerusalem, and they were all scattered throughout the regions of Judea and Samaria, except the apostles. Devout men buried Stephen and made great lamentation over him. But Saul was ravaging the church, and entering house after house,

he dragged off men and women and committed them to prison. Acts 7:59-8:3

Saul ravaged the church. He threw men and women into prison after seeking approval from the high priest of the synagogue at Damascus. Terrorizing Christians was intentionally planned and brutally carried out.

God stopped Saul in his tracks with His voice and blinding light on the road to Damascus. From the heavens, Jesus asked, "Saul, why are you persecuting Me?" Scales fell away from Saul's hard heart as he spent three days blind and in prayer.

Saul may have meditated on Stephen's powerful message. Did God work in Saul's heart through Stephen's words, "You murdered the prophets and the righteous one?" Did this word of God permeate every cell in Saul's body? Stephen's cry, "Lord, do not hold this sin against them," likely shaped every word of every letter Paul wrote and every sermon Paul preached.

Paul received Jesus' forgiveness for persecuting and murdering His children. Paul declared, boldly, that which he knew for himself, "In him we have redemption through his blood, the forgiveness of our trespasses, according to the riches of his grace" (Ephesians 1:7). "He has delivered us from the domain of darkness and transferred us to the kingdom of his beloved Son, in whom we have redemption, the forgiveness of sins" (Colossians 1:13-14).

Connect these words of Paul with being grafted into the vine and root. A branch, grafted into the flesh of the one true vine, lives "*in* Him." A branch, cut away from darkness, is "transferred to the kingdom of his beloved Son." Forgiveness flows and grows from our "grafted-in" resting place in Christ.

Paul humbly asked the disciples of Jesus for forgiveness; the disciples forgave him. We don't find the account in Scripture; however, it is also safe to say that Paul asked for forgiveness from those he persecuted and from the families of those he murdered. They forgave him because healed, growing children of the risen Lord forgive with God's forgiveness in Christ.

Paul developed many enemies as he preached Jesus throughout the world—Paul released to God the deep wounds and pain they caused him. God worked through Paul's story—all of it! The Holy Spirit prompted Paul to write these words for us,

> Put on then, as God's chosen ones, holy and beloved, compassionate hearts, kindness, humility, meekness, and patience, bearing with one another and, if one has a complaint against another, forgiving each other; as the Lord has forgiven you, so you also must forgive. And above all these put on love, which binds everything together in perfect harmony. Colossians 3:12-14

Grow in Faith and Forgiveness

The apostles cried out, "Lord, increase our faith" (Luke 17:5)! What words of Jesus stimulated this begging? Why did they need Jesus to grow, deepen, and expand their faith?

Jesus had just given them seemingly impossible instructions on forgiveness! Forgive, from your heart, seven times seven times—that number indicated infinity.

Immediately before the disciples begged Jesus to grow their faith, Jesus said, "Pay attention to yourselves! ("Be on your guard!")

NASB) If your brother sins, rebuke him, and if he repents, forgive him, and if he sins against you seven times in the day, and turns to you seven times, saying, 'I repent,' you must forgive him" (Luke 17:3-4).

We are called to forgive, in fact, required to forgive someone who asks for forgiveness. Our forgiveness must flow freely. "Be on guard; pay attention to yourselves," Jesus declared. Why?

A look at the prayer Jesus taught His disciples to pray provides insight: "forgive us our debts, as we also have forgiven our debtors. And lead us not into temptation, but deliver us from evil" (Matthew 6:12-13). Jesus forgives. We forgive because He forgave us. Our prayer? "Lord, increase our faith!" "Lead us not into temptation!"

Jesus knew the temptation we would face! The cry of our wounded soul may sound like this: "Jesus, forgive me, but don't ask me to forgive those who have hurt me."

Living without forgiving is not living. Living outside forgiveness halts healing and growth—a stunted, flailing faith results. Jesus calls our weary hearts to Himself, wraps us up in His love and mercy, and urges us to heal, grow, and forgive.

Forgiving infinitely is impossible! Yes, that is correct. In and of ourselves, it is impossible because the forgiveness we offer is not our own. It is God's forgiveness. We cry, "Lord, grow our faith!" Jesus declares to us, "What is impossible with man is possible with God" (Luke 18:27). Christ's forgiveness flowed fully and freely for all—we know that with our brain, but can our hearts embrace the call to forgive?

Our faith journey reflects many stories in the Scriptures:

forgiveness flows, and faith grows; faith grows, and forgiveness flows. Vine and vinedresser call forth mature fruit of faith and forgiveness.

Forgiveness is precisely where the rubber hits the road in our faith walk. We have the opportunity, most fully and ultimately, to live out our faith when we practice forgiveness and forgive those who are repentant. We heal when we forgive. We grow in faith and love when we take the courage to ask for and receive forgiveness.

Jesus cried out, "Father forgive them, for they know not what they do" (Luke 23:34a). Stephen implored, "Lord, do not hold this sin against them" (Acts 7:60). Jesus asks God to forgive them because He loves them; Stephen begs God not to hold their sin against them because he loves them. Jesus and Steven didn't say, "I forgive you," to unrepentant hearts.

We are not called to forgive apart from the repentance of those who commit evil against us. We are called to and required to forgive when someone asks for forgiveness. What, then, are we called to do when someone who has offended us doesn't repent? We are called to give it to God, just like Jesus and Steven. We are called to release judgment and justice into God's hands.

Our cry of faith mirrors Jesus' words, "Father forgive them" and Stephen's words, "Lord, do not hold this sin against them." We pray for our enemies.

Sadly, I've watched and experienced the sad misuse of Jesus' call to forgive. Perversion of the call to forgive can place individuals in extreme danger. Here are a few examples of dangerous teaching and misguided counseling.

"Forgive and forget" has been spoken to those who have endured trauma at evil hands. This further deepens the wounds of a wounded soul. Forgiveness is required if the offender has asked for forgiveness (maybe not to their face if it's not safe). Releasing the offense to God releases its hold on us. Forget, no way!

God doesn't forget our sins. He chooses not to remember them, and He chooses not to hold them against us. We don't forget the wrong. We release the wrongs as we give them to God. God heals our wounds and, by doing so, heals our memories. Our memory serves a purpose—to teach us, and prayerfully keep us from repeating previous mistakes.

Wounded individuals are often told that they must forgive and continue the relationship. The truth usually means releasing the offender by walking away. The wise pastor, counselor, or friend never puts the wounded in harm's way. Extreme danger can result from counseling a person to stay in a hurt-filled relationship.

It is essential to reflect on different types of repentance. Offenders often repent and show remorse when forced to suffer the consequences of their behavior. For example, an abuser says, "I'm sorry," while sitting in prison but returns to the same evil acts upon release. They may be sorry to have been caught and punished but not genuinely sorry for the hurt they have caused, nor willing or perhaps even capable to make necessary changes.

True repentance means to repent or say, "I'm sorry," accompanied by a genuine change of heart toward God and others. Repentance from the heart speaks, "I'm sorry. I regret my actions and will show you that I will make things right over a long period." The above examples are extreme cases where caution must be used. All of us sin and need forgiveness—all of us need Jesus to soften our hearts to His word and will in our lives.

These examples only scratch the surface of the plethora of ways God calls us to practice forgiveness and release offenses to Him. As unique as our fingerprints are our individual experiences with hurting others or being hurt, asking for and offering forgiveness.

By sacrificing the life of His perfect son, God gave His all. He richly and fully forgave then and continues to forgive now. Forgiveness heals and grows us! As we heal and grow, the vinedresser continues His work in us.

Forgiveness heals and grows us!

CHAPTER II

PROCESS WITH PURPOSE

My father is a vinedresser. I've watched his work and I've worked under his guidance. From this context, I write about the process of vineyard development and the annual work accomplished at their direction. As I write today, my son fills the vinedresser role in Steinbeck Vineyards. Trained and guided by my father his whole life, Ryan oversees our vineyards as our vinedresser.

The trellis structures are built in fields before planting baby vines. I knew the trellis' importance for training young vines. One year I saw a shoot of a branch strangled by being tied too tightly to the trellis. I've come to see that the rigid trellis system and training young vines can be likened to training under the law of God. The strangled little vine, tied too tightly, can be likened to one suffering under the misuse of the law.

Profound images appear through the process of thinning shoots and fruit. These likenesses will bring crystal clarity to Jesus' words, "Every branch in me that does not bear fruit he takes away" (John 15:2a).

Shoot thinning was one of the most straightforward images to connect with Scripture; pruning was one of the most challenging. I begged God to open my eyes and heart. Year after year, I watched pruners intentionally prune with sharp shears. Deeply wounded branches heal! Questions and prayers flow as we process the purpose of pruning.

May God bless our journey into the purpose of the process!

STUDY 7: THE VINEDRESSER AND THE VINE

My father is a vinedresser. He tends and gardens. Years of watching him work the vineyard provide a unique perspective of Jesus' words, "My Father is the vinedresser." I've watched my father work, and I mirror his work. The Scriptures have germinated in the soil of my heart, and the word of God has taken root and grown from this view. I've studied him while asking, "why?"

Why did Jesus say, "I am the vine; you are the branches, abide?" Why did Jesus say, "I am the true vine; my Father is the vinedresser?"

To help us answer that question, let's uncover more about the vinedresser in my life. He plants, trains, waters, and prunes 500 acres of vines in Steinbeck Vineyards. He assesses the needs and health of the vines. He takes action—spraying pests and weeds, ensuring sustainability and safety for our workers and families. He check the ripeness of fruit and harvest our crops when they mature.

More than just his work, the essence of his being is tied to the land and the vines. He is patient and prudent, precise and meticulous. He is vigilant and alert. The list goes on and on.

When you meet my dad, Howie Steinbeck, you must catch a glimpse of his hands. Scrutinize dad's hands as they rest on the steering wheel of the old Jeep. Observe as he touches the vines explaining this or that to you. Watch as he hands you a ripe cluster of grapes inviting you to taste and see. Weathered and worn, his hands paint a picture of the old school, salt of the earth, and hard work.

Dad began his career farming as a little boy as he walked alongside his grandpa Frank, mirroring his mentor's every move. His strong hands provided for a family of six and remodeled the historic ranch house grandpa Frank built in 1921. His hands changed the oil, dug irrigation ditches, and planted grapevines. Practical and rugged, he forged a path of vine growing long before it was in vogue in Paso Robles, CA.

The work of Howie's hands extends from his heart. Broken at the early death of his beloved grandpa Frank, grief overtakes his emotions, and his lips quiver as he talks about his grandpa. His hands and heart still work the fields, contributing to the vineyard business he built. He's proud; he's humble. He's tough and tender. He reveals his love for my mom, his family, and Jesus with great tenderness. The fourth of seven generations, he's attuned to the fact that three generations have gone before him, and three generations follow.

He's not a perfect vinedresser, like Jesus' Father, the vinedresser. He'd be the first to admit that he's not a fan of regulations and doesn't fully appreciate new viticulture practices until he sees them at work for a few years. He struggles with an aging body and the lack of strength to "get er done" like in years past.

My father faces challenges that any robust and self-made man faces. He doesn't like letting go of the reins, even though he's handing them off to his grandson, with whom he has worked for more than a quarter century. He can't sit still and needs to stay busy to feel fulfilled. Waiting for fields to dry out after a big storm causes restless angst.

My father cannot possibly accomplish the work of any season

on 300,000 vines single-handedly! There is too much work. He hires and trains workers to do the job. One lazy Sunday afternoon, my friend and I were on a vineyard walk between football playoff games. In the distance, we spotted a white truck. "Dad's doing something," I commented. Sure enough, my father had his large pruning shears in hand. He had pruned three vines, examples for the workers scheduled to arrive Monday morning. My vinedresser father works. Our workers follow his example and direction.

I learned that way too. I watched his work, and I worked. Following his example and training, I emulate his work ethic, his passion, his pride, and the practice of farming prime fruit.

Jesus' Father

Jesus, the vine, watched the work of His Father, the vinedresser. He worked the work His Father was working. After healing the crippled man on the Sabbath Day, Jesus declared,

> My Father is working until now, and I am working. For the Father loves the Son and shows him all that he himself is doing. And greater works than these will he show him, so that you may marvel. For as the Father raises the dead and gives them life, so also the Son gives life to whom he will. John 5:17, 20-21

What did Jesus do? He spoke life. He raised the dead. He healed the sick. He showered compassion on the crowds. Jesus did the work His Father chose to accomplish through Him.

Do you not believe that I am in the Father and the Father

is in me? The words that I say to you I do not speak on my own authority, but the Father who dwells in me does his works. Believe me that I am in the Father and the Father is in me, or else believe on account of the works themselves. John 14:10-11

The vinedresser's work was alive in Jesus because they were intimately connected. The present tense of that statement is also true: the vinedresser's work is active in Jesus because they are intimately connected. Jesus' work and His Father's work cannot be separated.

The vinedresser works; the vine works. Jesus continued,

Truly, truly, I say to you, whoever believes in me will also do the works that I do; and greater works than these will he do, because I am going to the Father. Whatever you ask in my name, I will do so that the Father may be glorified in the Son. If you ask me anything in my name, I will do it. John 14:12-14

I have felt that Jesus has bounced around Steinbeck Vineyards with me, in my old Jeep or on my tractor, speaking these words directly to my ears. He did, and He does! He is with me; he is in me, accomplishing His work. The same is true for you! Jesus is with you; Jesus is in you accomplishing His work.

Jesus also promised, "I will ask the Father, and he will give you another Helper, to be with you forever, even the Spirit of truth, whom the world cannot receive, because it neither sees him nor knows him. You know him, for he dwells with you and will be in you" (John 14:16-17).

*He is with you and with me—in me and
you, accomplishing His work*

I work the work God has placed before me—loving my family and neighbors and operating my business. While jumping in puddles with my grandchildren, fighting California water wars, and writing my heart in the quiet of the very early morning, I work. By His Spirit, whom He promised, He is with me and in me. The vinedresser and the vine work their work in me and work their work through me. The same is true for you, wherever you are called to bear fruit of the vinedresser and vine's work in you and through you.

We must continually focus on the vinedresser and the vine, at work for us and in us. If we take our eyes off that focus, we lose sight of mercy, love, healing, and growth, all of which flow from His hand.

Zealous religious leaders asked Jesus, "What must we do, to be doing the works of God" (John 6:28)? Knowing the thoughts of their hard hearts, Jesus didn't play along with their entrapment games. Jesus replied, "This is the work of God, that you believe in him whom he has sent" (John 6:29). God works faith. "Receive me, believe in me, trust me" was and is Jesus' work and word.

Receiving from The Vinedresser

Living and working as a daughter of a vinedresser, and watching dad's work over the seasons, taught me a meaningful sequence. Growing flows from receiving. Vines receive; vines grow. The fruit of receiving is growth; the product of receiving and growing is mature fruit. The eyes, hands, and heart of the vinedresser know the branches. He knows their needs, and his work meets those needs.

An essential need of growing branches is wounding. Branches must be wounded for proper growth to take place. Here are a few examples of the plethora of wounds intentionally inflicted by the vinedresser. In the spring, thinning creates a wound where excess shoots are removed from branches. Small clippers are used in late summer to remove small, unnecessary fruit clusters. Wounding occurs as fruit is cut off the branches with a sharp knife. Large pruning shears are the tool of choice as winter branches are pruned in preparation for the following year's growth.

Wounding is essential to growing and fruit-bearing—Ouch

We, branches of the one true vine, have been created by our creator to heal from wounds. We are fearfully and wonderfully made, beautifully designed to heal. As the vinedresser, He lovingly inflicts wounds by tending to the needs of branches.

There may be the temptation to race through the times we've been wounded and immediately associate those wounds with God's handiwork. The beautiful imagery laid before us through the vine and the vinedresser are enhanced by pausing, not by racing and immediately associating all wounding and pain with God's work.

God's wounding draws our attention to Him as the one who heals. Moses spoke a final song to the people, just prior to his death. He calls the children of Israel to trust God and to see Him as their rock and salvation. "See now that I, even I, am he, and there is no god beside me; I kill and I make alive; I wound and I heal; and there is none that can deliver out of my hand" (Deuteronomy 32:39).

Our perfect, holy God kills and makes alive, wounds, and heals. Job declared, "Behold, blessed is the one whom God reproves; therefore, despise not the discipline of the Almighty. For he wounds, but he binds up; he shatters, but his hands heal" (Job 5:17-18). God wounds and God binds up those wounds. The question Job wrestled with provides rich insights into the work of the vine and the vinedresser. Job's question paraphrased may sound like this, "Do we, as branches, trust God because all is well, or do we trust God because He is God?"

"The sword of the word of God," Simeon declared, "would pierce even the soul of Jesus' mother" (Luke 2:22-35). The word of God is likened to a sword that wounds: "For the word of God is living and active, sharper than any two-edged sword, piercing to the division of soul and of spirit, of joints and of marrow, and discerning the thoughts and intentions of the heart" (Hebrews 4:12).

The vinedresser knows what being wounded feels like. His heart broke as Adam and Eve disobeyed, hid, and blamed Him for their sin. His promise of a Savior flowed immediately into the hearts of these two broken human beings whom He had created for a relationship with Him. Wounds and the promise go hand in hand, then and now!

Peter knew in the depth of his soul that Isaiah's prophecy had been fulfilled right before his eyes in the wounding, death, and resurrection of his Lord.

> He committed no sin, neither was deceit found in his mouth. When he was reviled, he did not revile in return;

when he suffered, he did not threaten, but continued entrusting himself to him who judges justly. He himself bore our sins in his body on the tree, that we might die to sin and live to righteousness. By his wounds you have been healed. 1 Peter 2:22-24

Peter and Isaiah pointed to the cross, where God paved the path for all wounds to find context and meaning. Jesus, the perfect lamb of God, was abused and beaten, torn down by the hands God worked through to carry out His perfect plan. Redemption, restoration, and healing were worked on that day. The wounds Jesus received, that God allowed Him to endure, were for us. Thomas touched the scars of his risen Savior's hand, crying out the words we repeat, "My Lord and my God" (John 20:28).

Jesus carried the sin of the world, our sin, brokenness, separation from God, and death in His body to the cross. His death on the cross, days in the grave, and resurrection through the grave secured life for us. He conquered Satan, sin, and death in His body! Abiding in His work, we have conquered Satan, sin, and death in and through His holy life. Receiving God's wounding and trusting that healing will follow is the path of faith.

Wounds of this World

We live in this world. Living in this world, we experience deep wounds. The vinedresser heals any deep wounds we've endured! Some of the wounds we've encountered come through what we have done or left undone.

What has wounded you? Who has wounded you? What has broken your heart? Injustice? Infidelity? Fear? Failure? Death of a spouse or a child? End of a dream? The Psalmist cries out, "He heals the brokenhearted and binds up their wounds. He determines the number of the stars; he gives to all of them their names. Great is our Lord, and abundant in power; his understanding is beyond measure" (Psalm 147:3-5).

King David's faith amid deep trials guides our meditation, "When the righteous cry for help, the Lord hears and delivers them out of all their troubles. The Lord is near to the brokenhearted and saves the crushed in spirit" (Psalm 34:17-18). Psalm 34 allows us to see the vinedresser's handiwork through David's persecution. David foretold Christ's suffering and death while begging God to deliver him from perilous circumstances.

> The eyes of the Lord are toward the righteous and his ears toward their cry. The face of the Lord is against those who do evil, to cut off the memory of them from the earth. When the righteous cry for help, the Lord hears and delivers them out of all their troubles. The Lord is near to the brokenhearted and saves the crushed in spirit. Many are the afflictions of the righteous, but the Lord delivers him out of them all. He keeps all his bones; not one of them is broken. Affliction will slay the wicked, and those who hate the righteous will be condemned. The Lord redeems the life of his servants; none of those who take refuge in him will be condemned. Psalm 34:15-22

Faith cries out, "The Lord hears and delivers." What about Christians being massacred? We cry out, "What? Is that hearing and delivering?" What about the death of a baby, a mother, a wife, or a husband? "Why, Lord?" we mumble or scream out. "What about those who are abused and wounded by the person who once promised to cherish and love?" Lord, have mercy!

He heals the brokenhearted and binds up their wounds

In faith, the Psalmist David declared, "The angel of the Lord encamps around those who fear him, and delivers them. Oh, taste and see that the Lord is good! Blessed is the man who takes refuge in him" (Psalm 34:7-8)! "Taste the mature fruit of the word and work of God," invites the vinedresser. See that the Lord is good in good times as well as amid trials and traumas.

The vinedresser is not the source of evil; Satan is. Wounded by Satan's lies and crushed by their disobedience, Adam and Eve became the parents of all brokenness and sin. Through their genes, we are inheritors of pain and suffering. And we add our sin and brokenness to the gene pool. David confessed, "For my iniquities have gone over my head; like a heavy burden, they are too heavy for me. My wounds stink and fester because of my foolishness" (Psalm 38:4-5).

David's wounds stunk because of his foolishness. Like a little four-legged visitor comes calling in the middle of the night, leaving behind a pungent odor. The air feels heavy, thick like soup. It stinks. That's how David's wounds stunk. To top it off, David's sin also festered like an infected wound. David admitted that his own doing wounded his heart and spirit.

David cried, "I confess my iniquity; I am sorry for my sin" (Psalm 38:18). Abiding in the true vine includes owning this truth, "If we say we have no sin, we deceive ourselves, and the truth is not in us. If we confess our sins, he is faithful and just to forgive us our sins and to cleanse us from all unrighteousness" (1 John 1:8-9). We confess. God hears; God heals.

Wounds take many forms. Regardless of the source of the wound, healing takes place through the work of the vinedresser as we abide in the vine's life. The vinedresser wounds; the vinedresser heals. This world wounds; the vinedresser heals. We sin; the vinedresser forgives and heals. The vinedresser and the one true vine hold, keep, forgive, and heal in all circumstances.

The Vinedresser's Agony

The vine endured deep wounds. Our sin and the brokenness of this world inflicted Jesus' wounds. In the most significant exchange of all time, Jesus took the punishment we deserved in His body on the tree. By his wounds, we are healed. "For our sake he made him to be sin who knew no sin, so that in him we might become the righteousness of God" (1 Corinthians 5:21).

I've witnessed my father's agony on many occasions. God's agony exceeds that of my father exponentially! Things are not how God created them to be. Pain and sadness grip His heart. Like Jesus' cry at the death of Lazarus, God cries out with Martha, "death stinks!"

Jesus' death stinks another way for God, too. At just the right time in history, God sent His Son into this broken world to be broken and poured out as an offering, once and for all time (John 3:16-19, Galatians 4:4-6). God the Father inflicted wounds upon Jesus through the hands of those chosen by God to carry out His plan for us and our salvation.

The vinedresser's broken heart took form on that Good Friday many years ago—hours of darkness, an earthquake, and the tearing of the temple curtain.

God's heart breaks at the loss many have suffered at the hands of an earthly father. Their father tainted their ability to cry out in faith to a holy, righteous heavenly Father.

He hurts, too, when we choose not to cry out to Him with our pain. He knows that we, like Mary and Martha, cry aloud or whisper silently, "Lord, if you had been here...." He welcomes that cry of faith!

Indifference breaks God's heart. He can handle our pain, our anger, and our questions. Ask away! "Why, God, why?" "Where were you?" "How can this ever change?" God's heart breaks, too, when in pain we believe Him to be distant and callous. Cry it out, "God, why are you so far away?"

The love of the vinedresser vastly outweighs His agony and His broken heart! His power to heal wounds knows no boundaries! He provided and wounded His own Son for us so that we can approach Him in every circumstance—broken hearts longing to trust and wounded lives filled with hope that He fulfilled and fulfills His promises in us. The vinedresser heals.

STUDY 8: THE TRELLIS SYSTEM

The trellis system rises above the 300,000 vines in Steinbeck Vineyards. Our eyes are drawn toward the green vines, but once the structure is pointed out, you recognize that metal stakes and wires support every vine.

The vinedresser works preparing the land and providing the structure baby vines need to grow and thrive. But before any structure is placed in the ground, tractors must work the field. Only the top few inches of soil are tilled for grain, the crop of choice on this land for seventy-five years. Grape vines are deep-rooted, so the soil needs a different type of tilling.

The first piece of equipment to get to work is a huge Caterpillar track tractor. Imagine a tractor with long shanks on the back, ripping the soil five feet deep in one direction and three feet deep diagonal to that. The sights and sounds of that track tractor pulling long shanks through our harsh soils at one mile per hour is a sight to behold! If we were to stand one hundred feet away, we could feel the earth's rumble. Huge clumps of dirt surface from deep down as the land is stirred.

After the soil is ripped in two directions, we fire up our John Deere to pull the disc over the bumpy ground. This is a workout for the driver, usually my dad, who must hold on tight! After passing back and forth over the land in different directions with the disc, the soil is ready to build the trellis system.

God worked to prepare the land for Adam and Eve. Preparation of the soil in a vineyard takes place in specific stages, as did God's work of creation on day one, day two, and day three. Unlike land preparation and trellis building in our vineyards taking place in neat and organized stages, land preparation and structure in creation took place at God's word and work.

The trellis system is like God's laws. We might be tempted to think of the laws of God narrowly, as in the Ten Commandments. We'll get to those, but first, let's explore the laws of God in the context of land preparation in creation.

The very first word of God created light. God's spoken word, Jesus, speaks from the beginning of time as we know it. Jesus, the light, not created, spoke light into being. John makes this vital connection to God's design,

> In the beginning was the Word, and the Word was with God, and the Word was God. He was in the beginning with God. All things were made through him, and without him was not any thing made that was made. In him was life, and the life was the light of men. The light shines in the darkness, and the darkness has not overcome it. John 1:1-4

God created light in His first spoken act. Creating light initiated the very first law of God, the separation of light and darkness. "And God said, 'Let there be light,' and there was light. And God saw that the light was good. And God separated the light from the darkness. God called the light Day, and the darkness he called Night. And there was evening and there was morning, the first day" (Genesis 1:3-5).

Ponder God's word and work on day four. He separated day and night, seasons, days, and years. He set the sun in place to rule the day and the moon in place to rule the night:

And God said, "Let there be lights in the expanse of the heavens to separate the day from the night. And let them be for signs and for seasons, and for days and years, and let them be lights in the expanse of the heavens to give light upon the earth." And it was so. And God made the two great lights—the greater light to rule the day and the lesser light to rule the night—and the stars. And God set them in the expanse of the heavens to give light on the earth, rule over the day and night, and separate the light from the darkness. And God saw that it was good. And there was evening and there was morning, the fourth day. Genesis 1:14-19

Each of the first six days of creation included God speaking through His word as He prepared the land and created the laws associated with holding and sustaining creation. The culmination of His creation brought forth Adam, a man created in His own image, from the ground. God formed Adam from dust.

God gifted Adam with dominion and rule over the earth and the creatures of the earth. "Then God said, 'Let us make man in our image, after our likeness. And let them have dominion over the fish of the sea and over the birds of the heavens and over the livestock and over all the earth and over every creeping thing that creeps on the earth'" (Genesis 1:26).

Included in the gifts God bestowed on Adam and Eve was the command: "You may surely eat of every tree of the garden, but of the tree of the knowledge of good and evil you shall not eat, for in the day that you eat of it you shall surely die" (Genesis 2:16-17).

How can a command be a gift? Just like God setting creation

in place with rules and order was a pure gift, God put this law in place to keep order — a great gift to all. Here's the progression: God created. God, as creator, sustains creation. God is God, ruler over all. Man is God's creation, ruler over only that which God gifted him to rule over. God created Adam and Eve in His image to be the likeness of God. Adam and Eve were not created to be God. That's the gift; that's the order our creator intended.

Building the System

The trellis system in our vineyard provides structure to the branches and shoots of the vines. The trellis supports growth, but it is not growth. The trellis system bears the weight of the shoots; it is not the shoots. The trellis system takes the weight of the fruit; it is not the fruit. The law provides structure but not growth. The law offers support but is not the fruit.

A fascinating, time-consuming process takes place as we build the structure. The process takes considerable energy as well as time. Understanding a few stages will allow us to draw parallels with the process of God establishing the law over time.

Surveyors mark our empty, smoothed-out field at 100-foot quadrants, precisely according to the design prepared by our irrigation company. Two workers stretch a one-hundred-foot rope from one marker to the next. Marked at precise 10-foot intervals, the rope is pulled, and a team of men equipped with plastic table knives places one at each mark. Eventually, a stake will be pounded four inches to one side of the knife, and a vine will be planted at the knife.

Our irrigation company takes the next steps in this precise

process. They lay out the mainline, sub-main, pressure reducers, couplers, risers, and valves. A ditch digger digs a 40-inch-deep trench perpendicular to the direction of the vine rows. The mainline and sub main are laid into the ditch and buried so that a tractor passing over doesn't damage the thick plastic pipes. All pieces must be properly glued together, in the proper order, including being connected to the primary water source, our underground well. Once complete, we call this our "irrigation system."

End posts anchor the trellis structure. Four-inch heavy steel pipes are pounded at the ends of each row with a tractor that looks like a giant prehistoric dinosaur. The hydraulic battering ram pounds the ten-foot pipe halfway into the ground at a precise angle—bam, bam, in quick succession, driving the pipe five feet underground. Wire comes next. Large round bales of 14-gauge wire are placed on a trailer customized for our needs. The wire unwinds as a four-wheeled ATV pulls the trailer through the field. One man on each end ties off the wire. Other men on the team clip the first wire, the drip hose wire, to the steel posts about twelve inches above ground level.

A nameless homemade contraption is connected to the hitch of our trusty ATV. An old steel drum holds a large roll of one-half-inch black hose. The drum spins on a swivel as the quad pulls the drip line across the rows. Without this spinning contraption unwinding the hose, we would need to constantly untangle the drip hose.

The hose is tied to the end posts, connected to the riser in the middle of the field, and clipped to the wire. An emitter is punched into the hose, one at a time, at every spot marked by the plastic table knife. Flushing and testing the all-important water lines is the final step in our six-month building process.

Building a vineyard structure takes time. Every well-planned and executed step has a specific purpose, all toward providing structure and water for the baby vines we're ready to plant.

We will add additional trellis wires over the next few months. The stabilizing wire is positioned halfway between the vineyard floor and the top of the stake. It makes the overall structure strong. The cordon wire provides the wire onto which shoots are trained. We finish the trellis system by stringing "tuck wires" and fastening a "cross arm" to the tall stakes close to the top. This final stage provides the notches into which the "tuck wires" are placed. Tuck wires hold supple shoots in a vertical position.

The vinedresser directs each step of the process purposefully, keeping in mind the end goal—the structure onto which we train growing vines that will eventually bear the fruit load.

God's original, masterful design offered rich opportunities to honor God. A rigid structure entered the world because of Adam and Eve's disobedience. God put them out of the garden and placed an angel to guard the way to the tree of life.

> Then the Lord God said, "Behold, the man has become like one of us in knowing good and evil. Now, lest he reach out his hand and take also of the tree of life and eat, and live forever—" therefore the Lord God sent him out from the garden of Eden to work the ground from which he was taken. He drove out the man, and at the east of the garden of Eden he placed the cherubim and a flaming

sword that turned every way to guard the way to the tree of life. Genesis 3:22-24

Access to the tree of life for Adam and Eve came only through the promised Christ. For all who follow, access comes only through the blood of Christ, the perfect sacrifice. "Blessed are those who wash their robes, so that they may have the right to the tree of life and that they may enter the city by the gates" (Revelation 22:14).

Perfect Obedience

The image of my vineyard trellis system being likened to the law of God invites further unfolding. The commandments serve as the backbone of the trellis structure. Each command reveals God's character and also reveal the structure for a relationship with God and include rules for living in healthy relationships with our neighbors.

Piece by piece, God built the trellis system of the law, one law after another, with an invitation of blessing and the promise of a curse. Jesus summarized the whole law when He declared to the religious leaders,

> And he said to him, "You shall love the Lord your God with all your heart and with all your soul and with all your mind. This is the great and first commandment. And a second is like it: You shall love your neighbor as yourself. On these two commandments depend all the Law and the Prophets." Matthew 22:37-40

Jesus summarized Moses' words,

> You shall therefore love the Lord your God and keep his charge, his statutes, his rules, and his commandments always. You shall therefore lay up these words of mine in your heart and in your soul, and you shall bind them as a sign on your hand, and they shall be as frontlets between your eyes. Deuteronomy 11:1, 18

> See, I am setting before you today a blessing and a curse: the blessing, if you obey the commandments of the Lord your God, which I command you today, and the curse, if you do not obey the commandments of the Lord your God, but turn aside from the way that I am commanding you today, to go after other gods that you have not known. Deuteronomy 11:26-28

Jesus' instruction, "do this, and you will live," drives home the serious nature of every law God ever spoke and placed before all people of all time. God's demand for perfection falls squarely on you and me, too!

> And behold, a lawyer stood up to put him to the test, saying, "Teacher, what shall I do to inherit eternal life?" He said to him, "What is written in the Law? How do you read it?" And he answered, "You shall love the Lord your God with all your heart and with all your soul and with all your strength and with all your mind, and your neighbor as yourself." And he said to him, "You have answered correctly; do this, and you will live." Luke 10:25-28

Our holy God requires perfect obedience! Therein lies the

tension of the trellis system—end posts and stakes are pounded deep into the land, and wires are strung tight and clipped in place. We attach cross arms near the top of the stakes. They hold the tuck wires in place.

During the winter, when vines are pruned and resting, the stark visual of the trellis system cannot be overlooked—we see thousands of little crosses hovering above the resting vines.

Jesus, the vine, spread out his arms on the cross. The perfect lamb of God, Jesus Christ, perfectly and completely followed every law, and all commands God ever put in motion. He died being faithful to the laws God had set in place. No human ever took God's law more seriously!

> Do not think that I have come to abolish the Law or the Prophets; I have not come to abolish them but to fulfill them. For truly, I say to you, until heaven and earth pass away, not an iota, not a dot, will pass from the Law until all is accomplished. Therefore whoever relaxes one of the least of these commandments and teaches others to do the same will be called least in the kingdom of heaven, but whoever does them and teaches them will be called great in the kingdom of heaven. For I tell you, unless your righteousness exceeds that of the scribes and Pharisees, you will never enter the kingdom of heaven. Matthew 5:17-20

Jesus demanded that which is impossible—"keep the whole law perfectly, every single word." Impossible? Yes, impossible for you and me. In Christ, all is possible. Paul said, "But when the fullness of time had come, God sent forth his Son, born of woman, born under the law, to redeem those who were under the law, so that we might receive adoption as sons" (Galatians 4:4-5).

Jesus, the final sacrifice, was nailed to the cross in our place. He received the punishment the perfect law of God required for disobedience to the laws of God. The Roman guards lifted the cross and let it drop into a hole in the ground, dug to hold it upright. Dropping it into this position worsened the punishment, and eventually, the cross killed the guilty criminal.

The trellis system held Him there. Or did it? The nails through Jesus' hands and feet did not keep Him bound to the cross. Jesus chose to stay there to fulfill all righteousness. Jesus chose to endure even His Father's wrath and abandonment for us.

Meditate on the interaction between Jesus and Pilate as he delivered Jesus to His death. "Pilate said to him, 'You will not speak to me? Do you not know that I have authority to release you and authority to crucify you?' Jesus answered him, 'You would have no authority over me at all unless it had been given you from above" (John 19:10-11a).

The law was perfectly fulfilled in the sacrifice of the holy Son of God, a human born of Mary, to carry out every single command and demand of His holy heavenly Father.

At the very moment of fulfillment of the law and the sacrifice's completion, God's creation groaned! The earth quaked, and darkness filled the sky. The curtain in the temple was shredded as Jesus fulfilled the law and all righteousness.

The Tension In The System

Jesus' complete fulfillment of the law didn't nullify the law. What does this mean for you and me? We live in a holy tension, a balance. We are completely bound and perfectly freed by Christ's work. Everything our holy God demands, He provides to us in and through the perfect life, death, and resurrection of His Son.

The Apostle Paul, an expert in the law from childhood, lived zealously for the law. He murdered those grafted into Christ's life! Saul's work could be summarized: "Get back on that trellis system, submit to the law of God." "Reject Christ." "Reject His life for you and in you."

After coming to faith in Christ, Paul became a protector of growth and freedom. He proclaimed that the law has a purpose, just as the trellis has a purpose—to provide the structure on which the branches could be supported and grow. The trellis system, like the law, cannot and does not give life.

Paul addressed this very issue through these questions: "Let me ask you only this: Did you receive the Spirit by works of the law or by hearing with faith? Are you so foolish? Having begun by the Spirit, are you now being perfected by the flesh" (Galatians 3:2-3)? He continued, "Does he who supplies the Spirit to you and works miracles among you do so by works of the law, or by hearing with faith— just as Abraham 'Believed God, and it was counted to him as righteousness'" (Galatians 3:5-6)?

When solely focusing on and following the law, the only way is to obey the whole law, every single rule, perfectly. Paul said, "For all who rely on works of the law are under a curse; for it is written, 'Cursed be everyone who does not abide by all things written in the Book of the Law, and do them'" (Galatians 3:10). "Is the law then contrary to the promises of God? Certainly not! For if a law had been given that could give life, then righteousness would indeed be by the law" (Galatians 3:21).

The beautiful law of God trains, guides, and shows us our deep need for the healing word and work of Christ. The Psalmist cried out, "Oh how I love your law! It is my meditation all the day" (Psalm 119:97). And "Great peace have those who love your law; nothing can make them stumble" (Psalm 119:165).

The law, like the trellis system, provides structure so that growth is supported and flourishes. We live in this tension Jesus describes,

> If you abide in me, and my words abide in you, ask whatever you wish, and it will be done for you. By this my Father is glorified, that you bear much fruit and so prove to be my disciples. As the Father has loved me, so have I loved you. Abide in my love. If you keep my commandments, you will abide in my love, just as I have kept my Father's commandments and abide in his love. These things I have spoken to you, that my joy may be in you, and that your joy may be full. John 15:7-11

These profound words Jesus spoke are tied to abiding in His love, in Him, and keeping His commandments! Jesus bound the keeping of the commandments to His joy and our joy. How can keeping the law bring joy to Him and to us?

What do we do? Do we trust in our ability to keep the whole law perfectly? Do we trust that keeping the law saves us? If not, do we trust that just trying hard must be enough for God? No, we trust Jesus. We look to Jesus as the keeper of the whole law and the author of our faith,

> Therefore, since we are surrounded by so great a cloud of witnesses, let us also lay aside every weight, and sin which clings so closely, and let us run with endurance the race that is set before us, looking to Jesus, the founder and perfecter of our faith, who for the joy that was set before him endured the cross, despising the shame, and is seated at the right hand of the throne of God. Hebrews 12:1-2

As we grow, we are trained onto the trellis system by the loving hands of the vinedresser. Let's dive into the rich imagery, the process of the baby vines being planted in the soil, growing, and being trained up on the trellis system.

STUDY 9: TRAINING YOUNG BRANCHES

Our Jeep tour takes us to a field that looks more like a cemetery than a growing vineyard. The trellis system, complete with cross arms, hovers over tan-colored grow tubes that line up in perfect symmetry. The growth of the vines peeks over the top of the 24-inch tubes that protect the young vines from creatures and the elements.

"I want you to see how we train the young vines," I declare as I stop our classroom and invite you to hop out of the Jeep. Training the vines reminds me of the training we receive throughout our lives. "There are so many comparisons! Let's take a look."

I untie and remove the grow tube, revealing a small grapevine. I point out the graft union where the branch was grafted into the vine, the rootstock. "This baby has been in the soil of Steinbeck Vineyards for six months, and it's time to begin the training process."

I point to the buds, spaced at even intervals on this supple branch. There is a bud at every leaf, and from each bud shoots grow. A white truck stops at our Jeep, and dad hops out. "Good timing, dad. Can you show us the training process?" He eagerly grabs his clippers after I make quick introductions.

"We train every branch," dad says while touching the base of the young vine. "Look, the graft wound has become a scar, and the branch is growing from that point up. This little branch will be trained as the trunk of the vine. It is trained to this vertical stake, and when it reaches the cordon wire, we'll cut it off," demonstrates dad as he ties the green "tie tape" around the supple branch—not too tight so that the young branch can grow freely without being strangled.

"Why do you cut off the branch when it reaches this wire?" You ask, having a hard time comprehending wounding a growing branch! "There is an important reason," dad reflects. "We need lateral shoots. Look here," he says, pointing to the buds on the vertical branch, the trunk. "Our creator designed this perfectly! The buds alternate directions—this bud grows this way, the next bud grows that way," dad points out.

"Our trellis system is built for a 'bi-lateral' cordon, meaning shoots from the branch grow in two directions," flow these words from dad, the vinedresser's knowledge base. "We cut off the branch so that the shoots grow laterally and to stop the growth upward," he continued.

We climb in the Jeep you reflect, "Grape-growing is complex!" "Training a child is complex too," I reflect, thinking about the many parallels between training grape vines onto the trellis system and training up children. Tears well up as I think about my father talking to our guests about training branches of grape vines while I think about my childhood training!

Healthy Training

A newborn's cry trains astute parents. Parents begin training the child as the baby matures in an environment where basic needs are met. As grapevines grow, we train onto the trellis system. As a child grows, very complex development takes place over many years. Fruitfulness increases as individuals are cared for, disciplined, equipped, and instructed in all aspects of life. Spiritual training parallels the image of the trellis system being likened to the law of God and training likened to a conscientious parent training up a child.

The wise Solomon called parents and leaders to "Train up a child in the way he should go; even when he is old he will not depart from it" (Proverbs 22:6). The Psalmist declared, "Blessed is the man whom you discipline, O Lord, and whom you teach out of your law" (Psalm 94:12). The author of the book of Hebrews reflected, "For the moment all discipline seems painful rather than pleasant, but later it yields the peaceful fruit of righteousness to those who have been trained by it" (Hebrews 12:11).

To train is to alter the natural path. Wild grapevines sprawl, creep, and crawl! Likewise, children and adults, left to their hearts and nature, grow wild and unruly.

Training, discipline, and instruction in the law are necessary and proper—from the platform of consistent love and mercy! As we discussed through Paul's words in a previous chapter, the baby Christians in Galatia had been drawn to Christ through the good news of His perfect life, death, and resurrection. And then they reverted back to the law. Paul asked, "Did you receive the Spirit by works of the law or by hearing with faith? Are you so foolish? Having begun by the Spirit, are you now being perfected by the flesh" (Galatians 3:2-3)?

Jesus fulfilled the whole law perfectly. We abide in the vine. We are perfectly bound to the entire law and perfectly free to live alive, abiding in Christ's holiness. This truth must be part of healthy training.

Unhealthy Training

Many, perhaps with good intentions, make the law the primary message. Children and adults who hear Jesus' words, "Do this and you will live," more loudly and consistently than His words, "abide and breathe in freedom," live underdeveloped spiritual lives. Emphasizing the law would be like saying that the trellis system in my vineyard is the agent of growth or that which produces fruit. As we discussed, the trellis supports and provides the structure for freedom to grow, mature, and bear fruit.

Leaders and parents may be fearful that freedom will make one grow wild. They bind the one being taught tightly to the structure and speak the law as though life comes through the law. We must understand that the law serves an essential purpose—guiding, disciplining, and showing us our need for the Savior's work. The key word is "serve." The law serves, not the other way around.

Speaking the law without the overflowing love and mercy of Christ strangles, girdles, and restricts growth. "You are a sinner," while true, screams into ears hungry to hear and receive love and mercy. We may know in our mind that Christ forgives us, but that differs tremendously from intimately knowing love in our hearts and soul.

Voices from our past may scream, "you are not enough—be more, do more so that you can prove your value." Strangulation by unhealthy attempts at perfection must be cut off and retrained.

Retraining

Dad meets us in Phase 5 Cabernet to tell us an important story about a particular vineyard block. Dad began, "We planted this block in 1995. As the vines grew, we trained the branch up as the trunk and trained the shoots bi-laterally onto the wires." He continued with a concerned look on his face, "as these vines aged over the years, we noticed a steep decline in the health of the shoots and the quality of the fruit. Experts tested the soil and the leaves for imbalance or disease. Nothing was found."

"What could be wrong?" We asked ourselves. "Finally, we understood," dad said as he pointed to a piece of dead wood hanging on a wire. "When crews trained the shoots onto the cordon wire, they wrapped the supple shoot too tightly!" "Look," dad said, "the wire strangled the shoots!"

Sap flow was girdled and severely restricted by the wire. There was no possibility for healthy growth or mature fruit because sap wasn't flowing to every cell of the shoots. Rather than supporting the vine, the trellis system became death to the vine's shoots.

"You have to see this," dad declared. "We discerned that the rootstock and trunk were healthy. The shoots up to the point where the wire grew through them were healthy too." Excited, dad pointed out that our workers cut the wires and used a chainsaw to cut the cordon as close to the trunk as possible.

The following growing season, new shoots burst forth! "We chose the strongest shoot and, this time, tied it loosely to the new wire," dad concluded. The vine and branch were salvaged and now thrive. We paused, realizing the rich connections to our life experiences in this story!

How many of us, branches of the true vine, are restricted by training in the law we received as we were growing up? How many of us, knowing God's grace is a gift in our mind, can't hear or grasp hold of that clear message in our hearts? Who hears the discipline of their angry father or fire and brimstone being preached, therefore, cannot hear the love of God, the Father? Thankfully, many were trained by a loving father. Even if that is the case, some retraining may be necessary.

I am blessed with a father who embraces me and tells me he loves me. People love dad's genuine smile and sweet love for his land. Dad would be the first to tell you that he needs mercy and love to grow, just as we all need Jesus!

"We can be retrained!" I declare after jumping back into our Jeep. "Sometimes, retraining is a simple shifting of focus to receive the sap flow, the blood flow of Christ's redeeming work into every aspect of our being. However, sometimes deep cutting must take place at times to remove the deadness created by the law strangling our hearts and minds."

In my observation, even those trained in families that properly use the trellis system and urge growth need new growth and re-training! After bouncing toward our next stop, I quietly reflect, "keep in mind, branches and shoots of the vine don't complete this process for themselves—the vinedresser directs and oversees the work."

"You can talk to dad when he gets home" meant "you're in trouble," during a time in my early training. I wasn't a bad kid, just busy and challenging for my mom, who tended to household chores and managed my three siblings and me. Dad worked long hours to provide for our family, farming grain after his regular work day on our large ranch.

Today, many years later, Dad might leave a message on my cell, saying, "Cindy, this is Dad; call me back." I hear, "CINDY, YOU'RE IN TROUBLE. GO TALK TO DAD." I must pause, breathe, and re-think—"we work together today. Dad appreciates me for who I am. I didn't do anything wrong."

Multiply this way of thinking if we were to substitute God our Father for our earthly Fathers. Imagine its impact on hurting souls! Children and many adults may find it very hard to focus on the love and mercy of God, but in quiet moments of self-doubt and fear, the focus falls on the harshness and the law. This thinking permeates every cell of our being.

Jesus declared: "I am the true vine." We are grafted in, healed, and growing. Our whole being is called to live. We abide in the flesh of the vine, grafted in, healed by His wounds. Christ dwells in our hearts—cleansing us with His blood. The sap flows powerfully to every cell of the branch and shoots—carrying living water and nutrients to every cell in our body. The word of God calls us to retrain our way of being and doing.

Pause. Pray. Breathe in the pure breath of God! Father, Son, and Holy Spirit call us to grow in faith, hope, and love. The Triune God works non-stop, continually, intentionally for you and for me, in you and in me. Paul insists, "For freedom Christ has set us free; stand firm therefore, and do not submit again to a yoke of slavery" (Galatians 5:1). A healthy way of living and growing, rooted and grounded in love and mercy, flows from the work of the Triune God. The word calls you and me to live life alive!

The word calls you to live life alive

"Live life alive" flows beautifully, but what does it mean in every moment of everyday existence in practice? I pray that these examples of my early training and retraining experiences urge you forward in your faith walk. While our life experiences differ, I'm convinced we have much in common.

My early training did not develop the muscles necessary to think about how I think. As a result of this, coupled with a few unspoken traumatic events, I spent an inordinate amount of time thinking about how other people think. Confused inside, I attempted to ease my inner turmoil by figuring out the thoughts and emotions of others.

Retraining my heart to "think about how I think" took courage! I asked, "How do I think about God's word for me?" "How do I think about myself as a daughter of God?" I placed myself in the Gospel stories. "What am I blind to?" I asked, in the context of Jesus healing the man born blind. I looked at the courage of that man as he was confronted by religious leaders and thrown out of his place of worship for proclaiming Jesus' healing. The blind man's words became my own, "Lord, I believe," and I worshiped Him. (see John 9)

My early training taught me to be strong and independent. The "I can do it myself" stage toddlers express vehemently was not balanced with the skill to ask for help. I carried that mindset well into my adult years.

Learning to ask for help took place slowly! I needed to learn that God was calling me to allow others to work His work in me through others serving me. Serving others was comfortable for me, and I must admit, it provided a hiding place for my hurting heart. Being served was foreign; receiving was very uncomfortable.

God worked to retrain my heart and mind through a Christian therapist. My church training hammered into me this harsh, untrue statement, "Only people who don't have the faith that God will heal them go to therapists. God's word and forgiveness should be enough." I recall family members talking harshly about and mocking a "crazy cousin who was going to counseling." "Only crazy people in this family go to counselors" was a mindset I took as my own at an early age.

My early religious training did not clearly distinguish between guilt and shame. That, coupled with hearing "shame on you" when I did something wrong, locked a shame culture deep within my soul.

Retraining took time and a deep look at God's word! The "shame on you" culture originated in Adam and Eve's disobedience. That culture is alive and well in many hurting hearts; I've learned as I processed my shame. Ashamed at their nakedness, Adam and Eve hid from one another and God. I traced my tendency to hide in shame back to those moments in Scripture, and I no longer felt alone.

Shame binds one tightly to the trellis, restricting growth and freedom. Proper guilt says, "I've done wrong, God, please forgive me." Shame whispers into our ears and heart, "Not only did you do wrong, but you are wrong—simply for being." Strangulation by shame must be retrained.

Retraining took place slowly as God worked to move my faith from my mind to my heart. I've mentioned a few questions that played a vital role in waking up my strangled soul, heart, and spirit! I continue to welcome and ponder questions. Here are a few more questions: "Could it be that 'mid-life crisis' ensues because our early training taps out?" "What we learned in our early years has taken us this far. Is today the day we embrace a deeper learning journey that acknowledges that our whole being needs care—body, mind, spirit, heart, soul, and emotions?"

Calling On The Vinedresser

The vinedresser trained the vines. We cannot and do not retrain ourselves. God works retraining through His word. His light shines into dark places, and the living word urges us forward. Does this sound too simple to be profound? We know to the depth of our being that God's word was for others—we need to know, with our soul, into the depth of our being, that God's word and work are for me!

As God retrains us, our prayers shift. Not only do we pray for others, but we also pray for ourselves, our growth, and for our faith to develop and bear the fruit of abiding. We pray, "Thy will be done on earth as it is in heaven; Thy will be done, on earth, in me, as it is in heaven." "Lord, I believe, help my unbelief," flows from our hearts as does the cry, "Lord, help my deadness hear your call. Raise me, just like you raised Lazarus from the dead, please!"

Retraining is possible at the direction and hand of the vinedresser! Retraining, however, is not possible by doing the same things we've been doing over and over again. Looking back on our bumpy, not-in-any-way neat and tidy journey, we see God's hand at work in every step of the retraining, growing process. There are no laws, except the law of love, governing the journey and our growth! The fruit of the Spirit grows out of Christ's work for us and in us and our life grafted into His life.

To be retrained, we need to think differently. We receive and rest while abiding *in* the life of the one true vine. *In* Him, we are trained to trust that the law was fulfilled in His life, death, and resurrection. He opens our blind eyes and deaf ears; Jesus heals our hearts, soul, spirit, mind, and bodies in and through His life.

STUDY 10: THINNING SHOOTS AND FRUIT

We've likened preparing a field and building the trellis system to the law of God. The image of training young vines gives us pause to honestly assess aspects of our early training and ponder our need for retraining. In this study, we'll consider the all-important thinning process in our vineyard and how these seasons relate to our lives.

Understanding the difference between a branch and the shoots is essential to this image. For grafting, we cut away a single bud to graft into the rootstock. The scar on the trunk made by grafting jumps out as I point to the thousands of wine and branch scars. The branch begins just above the soil, and it's trained up as the trunk and then trained to bi-laterally cover this wire. We call the growth unfolding out of these buds the shoots.

Jesus is the vine and the root, not the branch or the shoots. We're the branches, trained onto the trellis system, and our lives produce the shoots and fruit that freely grow from the branch. Shoots are thinned mid-spring, and fruit is thinned mid-summer.

The vinedresser plucks away excess growth and weak shoots to achieve the highest quality in the vineyard. Through thinning imagery, we explore the importance of the vinedresser thinning away any immature non-prime fruit. "Growing shoots and abundant fruit is the goal," we cry out, wondering how wounding by cutting away shoots and fruit can be beneficial.

Our connection as a branch in the vine remains our primary focus as we unfold the vital work of the vinedresser thinning shoots and fruit. Nothing takes place outside that connection, as

Jesus said, "Every shoot in me that does not bear fruit he takes away" (John 15:2a). This question is important, "If a shoot is *in Him,* why would it need to be taken away?" Another substantial question we'll address is, "Isn't all fruit growing from shoots of a branch good fruit?"

When we cut off excess shoot growth and fruit growth, cuttings are dropped to the ground. The leaves, shoots, and fruit become rich mulch. "Nothing is for nothing," I reflect as I start up our Willys Jeep.

Thinning Excess Shoot Growth

This warm day in mid-May is perfect for our Jeep ride! I stop in a block of five-year-old Cabernet vines, driving a few vines down the row before stopping the Jeep. After pausing for a photo shoot of this unique perspective, I pull off a couple of green shoots growing from one bud. The first shoot is the smallest and doesn't have any fruit on it. The second shoot is a bit longer and grows a tiny cluster of Cabernet.

We look closely at the shoot left on the branch. These are the two prime clusters of fruit we want to mature for harvest in October. One single bud and every bud on the shoots has the possibility to grow the following:

- The primary shoot is the first shoot to burst out from the bud in the spring. The prime shoot produces two clusters of fruit, the prime fruit.

- The second shoot unfolds a week or two later and carries one cluster, a secondary cluster, smaller in size and weight.

- The third shoot unfolds from this one bud even later and bears no fruit. Its primary purpose would be vine-sustaining if frost were to kill the first two shoots.

You reach out, confident enough to thin a few shoots. We move down the row, thinning the excess shoots. As we look back, we see the sunlight filtering through the strong prime shoots. We pause to reflect on one single bud.

I hand you a tiny bud I've cut away from a shoot. Wound up inside each, and every bud is all shoot and fruit growth for the new season. A cross section of a bud placed on a microscope reveals next year's crop to a knowing eye. As growth bursts forth, we will witness the shoots and fruit held tightly in the bud as it unfolds. First, the shoots and then the tiny fruit forms become visible.

The second and third shoots must be thinned. Surplus shoot growth impedes light and wind flow. Before we thin, the shoots look like a jungle. After we thin even spacing between shoots and light gently filters through the growth.

The energy that would have been spent growing the shoots can now flow to the primary, strong shoot. The excess growth now lies on the ground creating all-important mulch.

We thin for another fundamental reason. We're positioning the shoot growth so that pruning efficiency improves for the following winter. The shoots are evenly spaced and positioned vertically. The primary shoot grows straight up while the secondary and third shoots grow out of the bud at more of an angle.

How can Jesus' words, "Every shoot in me that does not bear fruit he takes away" (John 15:2a), impact growing and bearing mature fruit? How does the vinedresser work in our lives to thin and position shoots?

Mary and Martha's story provides rich material as we unfold the images of shoot thinning and how it relates to our faith journey.

> A woman named Martha welcomed him into her house. And she had a sister called Mary, who sat at the Lord's feet and listened to his teaching. But Martha was distracted with much serving. And she went up to him and said, "Lord, do you not care that my sister has left me to serve alone? Tell her then to help me." But the Lord answered her, "Martha, Martha, you are anxious and troubled about many things, but one thing is necessary. Mary has chosen the good portion, which will not be taken away from her."
> Luke 10:38-42

Imagine how heartbroken Martha must have been as Jesus sided with her sister! Before imagining that, however, we must pause at Martha's boldness in involving a house guest in her frustration with her sister! Jesus must have been a trusted friend.

Sitting at the feet of a teacher, as Mary chose, was counter-culture and offensive to Martha. A famous guest graced their presence in their home. "We must serve Him," Martha reasoned aloud.

Mary understood Jesus' intention that day and was eager to receive, setting aside all training to the trellis of tradition and law she had previously received. Jesus came to serve, in their home, on that day. What did He offer? He extended the word of life. He gave Himself as the bread of life and living water. Mary received.

Martha's discomfort in receiving from Jesus plagues us! Jesus thinned those shoots in her, and He calls us to allow Him to thin those shoots from our lives. He turned her heart and mind toward Him by calling her to recognize her inability to pause, hold still, and listen. He focused her attention, naming precisely what got in the way—an anxious, troubled heart.

Martha's serving wasn't wrong; her timing was wrong. At that moment, Jesus called her to receive from him, not serve Him.

Excess shoots are not bad. However, they can get in the way of the prime shoots receiving all the energy and focus.

In another account, Martha hosted a meal for Jesus after Jesus called her brother Lazarus back to life—Jesus received her service and ate the meal that day. Jesus also received Mary's service that day.

> Six days before the Passover, Jesus therefore came to Bethany, where Lazarus was, whom Jesus had raised from the dead. So they gave a dinner for him there. Martha served, and Lazarus was one of those reclining with him at table. Mary therefore took a pound of expensive ointment made from pure nard, and anointed the feet of Jesus and wiped his feet with her hair. The house was filled with the fragrance of the perfume. John 12:2-3

Thinning excess shoot growth imagery gives us pause. What can we learn about focus and discernment? What can we uncover about the grief we experience as we let go of the prized shoots we've grown? Can joy flow out of the thinning process?

Focusing on God's work thinning excess growth allows me

to pause and ask, "what causes me to be anxious?" Go back one more time to the grafted into Christ imagery. We are the tiny little bud, the branch grafted into Christ's life. Wound up in every one of us lies all the shoot growth we will ever grow in our lives. The call on our heart and life is to allow the vinedresser to focus our growth and position us for the following years.

> *The call on our heart and life is to allow the vinedresser to focus our growth.*

Discernment plays a massive role in our lives. Unlike the vines and branches in my vineyard, we don't have a vinedresser overseeing and positioning our growth and the thinning process. Or do we? "What troubles me? What troubles you?" Jesus urges us to ask. We abide *in* the vinedresser's Son, and the Son abides in us, giving us insight and courage.

We live *in* the word of God. We're called to prayer, to ask for wisdom as we discern God's hand as He takes away excess growth to allow light and wind to flow in and through our lives.

Grieving the loss of the shoots we'd so exuberantly grown provides an opportunity for light to filter into darkness. We are wounded by shoots being taken away! This wounding allows the sap to work, healing the small wound quickly. With 20-20 hindsight, we can see the vinedresser's shoot thinning as healthy, even though we may have battled to maintain all growth.

Joy flows as light filters through the shoots, positioned to bear prime fruit. Paul invited, "So as to walk in a manner worthy of the Lord, fully pleasing to him: bearing fruit in every good work and increasing in the knowledge of God; being strengthened with all power, according to his glorious might, for all endurance and patience with joy" (Colossians 1:10-11).

We watch shoot thinning and participate with our hands. We see the jungle before and the clean positioning after. We smell decomposition as the tiny shoots shrivel and become part of the ground. Shoot thinning has rich parallels, so we pray for understanding for us, personally. What is God, through the vineyard, trying to teach us?

Do we fight the shoot-thinning process, preferring jungle to light and airflow? Fear of letting go of that which gives us safety and comfort might paralyze our minds. Slowly, God works to remove weak shoots and excess growth. That which might have been good was weak and unfocused, hidden under the guise of strength, and we've got this mentality.

What shoots did the hand of the vinedresser remove, slowly and tenderly in me? God thinned away the shoots of busyness. He removed the shoots of trying to serve everywhere. God thinned the shoots of needing to get things done right now. He positioned me to receive. God positioned me to live life balanced and alive.

God continues to work that work—every day of every year.

The light and airflow give us the courage to embrace God's masterful creation of our whole being—body, mind, soul, heart, spirit, and emotions. Light flows through, allowing us to see God at work, positioning us in Him to bear prime fruit into the future. We learn and continue to grow in the understanding that we need focus and discernment.

The thinned shoots of our lives fall to the ground and decompose into rich mulch. We grieve the losses, and God turns sorrow into joy. We recognize that God works for our good as He thins away shoots that take energy away from the prime fruit-bearing shoots.

Fruit Thinning

Our Jeep tour in early August takes us to Cabernet Sauvignon vines. Vine balance may necessitate the removal of clusters. Secondary clusters are removed in mid-May when we shoot thin. Most years require additional fruit thinning, so we achieve quality and balance.

This prime cluster of fruit is significantly behind in ripeness, so I cut it off. You gasp at my swift cut! "It has to go—look, all the berries were bright green. Compare that cluster to the deep, reddish-purple berries on the clusters hanging from the shoots. We want ripeness, quality, and balance in our wines."

Understandably, tiny secondary clusters are cut off, but it's shocking that big clusters are cut off. Everything we cut off falls to the ground and creates rich mulch—nothing is for nothing!

Jesus' disciples lived the fruit-thinning process with Jesus. "Follow me," invited Jesus. Luke recorded, "Jesus said to Simon, 'Do not be afraid; from now on you will be catching men.' And when they had brought their boats to land, they left everything and followed him" (Luke 5:10-11). James and John, Simon's partners in the fishing business, followed too.

The same goes for the one Jesus named Matthew, "After this he went out and saw a tax collector named Levi, sitting at the tax booth. And He said to him, "Follow me." And leaving everything, he rose and followed him" (Luke 5:27-28). Twelve men followed Jesus, and women followed too. Luke wrote,

> Soon afterward he went on through cities and villages, proclaiming and bringing the good news of the kingdom of God. And the twelve were with him, and also some women who had been healed of evil spirits and infirmities: Mary, called Magdalene, from whom seven demons had gone out, and Joanna, the wife of Chuza, Herod's household manager, and Susanna, and many others, who provided for them out of their means. Luke 8:1-3

Men and women followed Jesus, also, by staying home! They received Jesus' call to follow Him and stayed home to witness. Many, including myself, were trained to think that somehow bearing fruit means "big, bold, perfect fruit." Some believe that bearing fruit by serving at church or going on a mission trip is the only fruit that matters to God. This is not accurate in any way!

Look closely at Paul's words, "For we are his workmanship, created in Christ Jesus for good works, which God prepared beforehand, that we should walk in them" (Ephesians 2:10). Let's rephrase Paul's simple statement, God prepared good works, in advance, that we should walk in the fruit He's called us to bear. Think back to the buds on the shoots—wound up inside is all the fruit growth. It's there. As it unfolds and develops, immature or underripe fruit must be thinned. That's life. Simple, but far from simplistic.

Here are some rich parallels this fruit-thinning imagery provides. We want balanced, quality fruit. Wisdom develops as we open up our lives, submitting to and giving the vinedresser access to cut away immature, underdeveloped fruit.

The eyes and heart of the vinedresser and the vine urge us to more—not necessarily more fruit, but prime fruit. God's call is that we bear much prime fruit of abiding in His Son's life. Like second and third shoots, secondary clusters and unripe fruit must be thinned and go on the ground.

Quality necessitates careful discernment—too much fruit stresses the vine, and too little fruit and the vine isn't accomplishing what it was created to do. Quality vines live and produce prime fruit for thirty, forty, and even fifty years. Quality is achieved through balance.

In wisdom, the vinedresser cuts away fruit so that focus rests only on the prime fruit to which we are called. Wisdom ushers in the courage to ask questions; wisdom brings clarity. We pause and ask, "How is God growing discernment in us so we can properly distinguish prime fruit from secondary fruit? Where is God calling us to focus on growth and fruit?"

Permission grants our hearts access to complex questions and gives us courage. Inviting, rather than fleeing challenging questions, becomes the norm for our lives. Here are a few questions: Do we say yes to requests for the right reasons? Does saying yes detract from the prime fruit to which God has called us? Do we give ourselves permission to say no?

We pray for understanding. We beg God to show us His work in us. We observe the colors of the fruit change, witnessing underripe fruit and secondary clusters. We smell decomposition as immature fruit shrivels and becomes mulch on the ground. What is God teaching us?

Oh, we might bear fruit, loads of it—fruit here, fruit everywhere! We need the hands and heart of the vinedresser thinning the unripe, immature fruit. Paul's words open our eyes and heart to the profound simplicity and vast depth of God's call:

> For by grace you have been saved through faith. And this is not your own doing; it is the gift of God, not a result of works, so that no one may boast. For we are his workmanship, created in Christ Jesus for good works, which God prepared beforehand, that we should walk in them. Ephesians 2:8-10

We may have been raised to focus solely on verses eight and nine—"by grace through faith, a gift, not by works." While so true and correct that God's mercy is a gift, verse 10 is often completely and sadly ignored. Was overlooking good works intentional? Apart from our position of abiding in Christ's life, it is impossible to accurately teach verse ten, "We are his workmanship, created in Christ Jesus for good works, which God prepared beforehand, that we should walk in them" (Ephesians 2:10).

We may view others as His workmanship and His masterpiece. Are we able to believe this "for me?" Can we beg God for the courage to speak verse 10 this way: "I am his workmanship, His masterpiece, God's creation unlike any other in the world! I was created *in* Christ Jesus to bear the fruit God placed in me. I need to open my eyes and walk in the fruit, the good works right in front of me."

As branches of the true vine, we're called to learn and grow in our understanding of abiding *in* the vine. The hand of the master vinedresser has prepared all of the fruit of our lives, every bit we will ever bear in advance.

Let's look around carefully and courageously. What fruit has God prepared beforehand, for you, in you to walk in? Prime fruit, on which we focus our energy, becomes more apparent. Secondary and third clusters are recognizable too. The fruit we are called to bear is right in front of us. We are called to walk in it, not robotically but freely and fully.

Walking in the fruit God has prepared for us means learning to take care of our being and our heart, soul, mind, spirit, body, and emotions. God calls us to allow Him to remove the immature fruit, the imbalance of caring for others while not knowing how to care for ourselves. Slowly, as God removes the underripe fruit, we grasped how to ask for help. The vinedresser created us to bear the fruit of caring for our lives as well as for others.

We continue to learn to discern. We say no with grace, thankful for opportunities to bear fruit. We continue to learn to determine when to say yes. Saying yes and no more confidently and fervently flows from discernment.

Wounding — A Process with Purpose

Wounding hurts! Shoot and fruit thinning create necessary wounds on the tender shoots. Our loving vinedresser, knowing all things about sap flow and the blood of His Son in us, knows that His wounding provides opportunity after opportunity for healing. The vinedresser wounds; the vinedresser heals. He wounds precisely and purposefully.

Our loving vinedresser, knowing all things about sap flow and the blood of His Son in us; He knows that His wounding provides opportunity after opportunity for healing.

Sap flows rapidly to the tiny wound created by removing excess shoots. Sap flows quickly to the wound made by clipping off clusters of fruit. These wounds heal quickly. Growth and fruit that falls and becomes mulch on the ground are also part of the vinedresser's design. Supple growth and fruit lying on the ground decomposes, providing nutrients to the soil. Beneficial bugs and worms that live in the soil benefit too.

The focused energy of the healed branch and shoots flows freely, delivering nutrients and water to the primary growth. Excess shoots or fruit no longer steal away vitality. Energy is focused only on primary shoots and fruit for the remainder of the season until the fruitful harvest arrives.

These images challenge those of us who enjoy jungles! Many crave the chaos of chasing around growing shoots and bearing fruit here or there. But do we thrive, and live alive, when we run from the intentional wounding of the hand of the vinedresser desires? Shoots of branches must be purposefully thinned for ripe, mature fruit to develop. Fruit must be purposefully thinned too.

The vinedresser thins the shoots and fruit just as the vinedresser grafts us into the vine. The branch receives training on the trellis system from the vinedresser. He reminds us that the trellis is there for structure, but it doesn't bring health or growth. The shoots and fruit are not trained; they grow and produce freely while submitting to shoot thinning and fruit thinning at the hand of the vinedresser. We receive each of these practices—grafting and training, shoot thinning, and fruit thinning.

Relying on our energy and strength to fulfill the needs and necessary work creates unhealthy wounds. Attempting to do this work ourselves creates dysfunction. Depression thrives in that unhealthy wounding.

Trusting God's hand as He wounds, with purpose, and heals completely with mercy, drives our hearts even more deeply into the relationship He has created for us *in* Christ.

The incredible paradox of life *in* the vine is this: Abiding bears the fruit of our relationship with Christ. We're called to rest, receive, and be. These action words flow and grow from our position *in* Christ. From our position of being, we bear much fruit.

> *May God grant us the courage to ask for discernment and wisdom. May God provide loving outside eyes, hands, and hearts to usher us along in bearing the mature fruit of abiding.*

STUDY II: PRUNING

Pruning parallels pose a weighty mystery, one that deserves caution and humility. Watching and processing pruning for over a quarter century, one winter after another revealed what we will share in this study. I still and always will beg God for a deeper understanding of Jesus' pensive words, "Every branch in me that does not bear fruit he takes away, and every branch that does bear fruit he prunes, that it may bear more fruit. Already you are clean because of the word that I have spoken to you" (John 15:2-3).

Pruning takes place during the winter, a four-month season of rest. The vinedresser cuts back almost all the shoot growth from the current year so that the buds on the mature shoots protruding from the cordon can produce the shoots and fruit for the following year. Shoots containing buds that would produce fruit are cut off so that prime fruit grows. The growth that is cut off is chopped into small pieces and becomes rich mulch on the floor of our vineyard.

A pruning definition from the vineyard and Scriptures I've developed is simple: "Pruning cuts away that which could be good for that which is better." Pruning cuts away good shoots while leaving well-positioned buds that will produce prime fruit. I'll unfold my discoveries, unearthed only after years of studying the Scriptures and the vines, as well as watching my father prune our vineyard.

> *Pruning cuts away that which could be good for that which is better.*

Defining and understanding what pruning *is not* will serve us well as we dive into this study. Pruning is not discipline. Trauma or something terribly wrong happening in life is not pruning. Many authors I've read place pruning into the categories of God's discipline or the impact of negative life circumstances. While other Scripture verses speak of God's discipline or the effect of life, Jesus' words here speak specifically of pruning as it relates to His work of bringing us to bear more fruit and cleansing us.

Durning vineyard pruning, the vines are in a season of deep rest. Taken to a logical conclusion, comparing pruning to our lives fails at this point because we generally don't have a four-month season of rest like that in the vineyard. We have, however, previously stated that Jesus is our rest and in him we receive pruning. During the seasons of dormancy, the stillness of winter, and bare nakedness before God, the vinedresser prunes. As we will uncover, pruning places our focus solely on Christ, in Christ.

Wounding — A Process with Purpose

We were here in October, and the vines were green and growing! Now, these vines look dead. We had tasted ripe fruit and watched harvest from the Jeep on a warm fall day. Today we bounce around the vineyard bundled up on this day to combat the brisk January cold. Today's sights and sounds are vastly different from that October day.

"These vines are dormant," I reflect from the driver's seat of our Jeep. "Far from being dead, even though they look dead, the vines are sleeping for the winter, like a hibernating bear, vines rest. For four months, the leafless, bare vines conserve and store energy for the impending bud break in the spring."

During the season of rest, the roots still take in water and nutrients from the soil. The water and nutrients are transferred to all cells, albeit more slowly than during other seasons. I pause and ask, "Have you experienced a time in your life that looks like this—a season of being vulnerable and naked before God?"

"Frost," I continue, "causes the sap flow of the plant to retreat from the leaves. Once the energy draws back, the leaves turn brown and fall to the ground." Only three-foot-long bare shoots remain, blowing in the winter wind. What a sight! Three hundred thousand resting, naked grape vines surround us.

Up a gentle hill and around a corner, we spot my father's truck parked on the side of the road at a Cabernet Sauvignon block. "Dad's pruning," I reflect as we hop out of the Jeep to look closely. Dad joyfully takes over the conversation. "Each bud on this shoot and every shoot you see contains the shoot and fruit growth for the following year." He continued pointing to the evenly spaced little buds, "We must cut away almost all this growth from last year. We cut the shoots back, to here, he describes while touching two small buds."

"If we didn't prune, all these buds, each containing next year's crop would burst forth in the spring!" He said, and continued, "fruit would grow everywhere! Pruning concentrates the growth of the prime fruit."

Sharp shears in hand, he masterfully demonstrates pruning an entire vine. Unlike the tender shoots being thinned by hand, pruning makes deep cuts. The wounds are visible and take a considerable amount of time to heal. With purpose and precision,

Dad cuts away almost all of the shoots on that vine. He leaves eight spurs per cordon, and sixteen spurs per plant.

Each bud will produce one prime shoot and two fruit clusters. Sixteen spurs times two buds equal 32 buds per vine. Thirty-two buds equal sixty-four clusters per vine. That amount yields about four bottles of wine per vine.

"You hand prune all of these vines?" You exclaim as you wave your hand over the whole vineyard! "Well, I don't, but our workers do," Dad casually continued, not realizing the magnitude of awe in your mind as you see pruning for the first time.

Dad continued, "All shoots I cut off get chopped up into small pieces and remain on the vineyard floor. They create mulch over the years as they are worked into the soil. The cuttings become fertilizer and a home for the beneficial bugs." He turns to prune another vine. We thanked him and jumped in the Jeep to continue our tour.

Pruning = Cleaning & Positioning

After a quiet reflection, while coasting quietly, I quote Jesus' words, "Every branch that does bear fruit he prunes, that it may bear more fruit." Jesus didn't stop there. He said, "You are already clean because of the word I have spoken." Pruning equals cleaning and positioning.

We sit in my old Jeep, high above my vineyard, parked on Oma's Hill, as I begin unfolding the rich meaning of Jesus' words. I visualize Jesus teaching his disciples about pruning a vineyard during their walks from town to town. Jesus' disciples may have heard about positioning or cleaning up the previous year's growth from their teacher repeatedly! The apostle John carefully and intentionally recorded Jesus' words for us.

The word "prune" means to cleanse and purify. In Hebrews 10, the author proclaims Jesus as the fulfillment of the law, who "cleansed" by giving His perfect life as the final sacrifice. How does He continue to prune and cleanse the sinner? By His word that is sharper than any two-edged sword (Hebrews 4:12).

With a sharp tool and much healing involved, the vinedresser grafted us into His Son's life, and He continues His work, positioning the growth we bear so that we bear much fruit. We are already cleansed and clean because of the word Jesus has spoken. Pruning is the continued process of cleaning and purifying—through His word so that we bear prime fruit. The vinedresser continues His work on us, the branches, doing the work already completed in Christ! "It is finished," and His work continues.

Jesus speaks of the necessity of branches being pruned while speaking of the work He will accomplish in just a few short, agonizing hours. Jesus intimately connected His life work, including His upcoming suffering, death, and resurrection, to the fulfillment of the whole law. He also connected His suffering, death, and resurrection to His continual work in us. The author of Hebrews summarizes the vulnerability of pruning and the healing help we received through the word that wounds us and makes us alive.

> For the word of God is living and active, sharper than any two-edged sword, piercing to the division of soul and of spirit, of joints and of marrow, and discerning the thoughts and intentions of the heart. And no creature is

hidden from his sight, but all are naked and exposed to the eyes of him to whom we must give account. Since then we have a great high priest who has passed through the heavens, Jesus, the Son of God, let us hold fast our confession. For we do not have a high priest who is unable to sympathize with our weaknesses, but one who in every respect has been tempted as we are, yet without sin. Let us then with confidence draw near to the throne of grace, that we may receive mercy and find grace to help in time of need. Hebrews 4:12-16

This mystery places us at the mercy seat of Christ. We are completely clean in Him, and He prunes us by His word so that we will bear more fruit. The vinedresser wounded His son; the vinedresser precisely and purposefully wounded and wounds us. The wounds He makes position and cut back shoots (branches) that are already clean in Him. Grafted into Christ's life, rooted and grounded *in* Him, we are clean, and the word wounds us further so that we bear more prime fruit.

Lazarus, Mary, and Martha provide a rich example of pruning. First, Lazarus' death wasn't God's hand pruning—death is not pruning! Recall my definition of pruning: "pruning cuts away that which is good for that which is better." Death is punishment for Adam and Eve's sin, and we will pass through it because of their disobedience.

Pruning took place in the conversations Mary and Martha engaged in with Jesus after their brother's death. "Lord, if you had been here" is a journey cry. "Why" is a pruning cry. Mary and Martha trusted Jesus enough to make that statement and ask that question. Jesus pruned away good trust! Why? For more trust and a deeper faith in Him.

Jesus' question, "Do you believe this?" is a pruning question. Mary and Martha believed in the resurrection of the dead! They believed that their brother's resurrection would take place one day in the future. In essence, Jesus declared, your brother's resurrection will take place today, through me.

> Jesus said to her, "Your brother will rise again." Martha said to him, "I know that he will rise again in the resurrection on the last day." Jesus said to her, "I am the resurrection and the life. Whoever believes in me, though he die, yet shall he live, and everyone who lives and believes in me shall never die. Do you believe this?" John 11:23-26

Martha's belief in the resurrection on the last day was good fruit from previous growth. Jesus pruned away good growth to clean and position her life for focused growth and the best fruit. Do we believe that we have died and that our life is hidden in Christ? Christ is the resurrection and the life, ours, now, today.

The stone in front of Lazarus' tomb was good because it kept death in. The good stone that kept the stink of dying and death in the tomb impeded Jesus' work. When Jesus told them to "take away the stone," they accurately declared that their brother's body stunk. Jesus said, yes I know, death stinks. Jesus' words, "Take away the stone," pruned them. They were already wounded by Lazarus' death, and now they would be wounded more by removing the stone and seeing their brother's lifeless body. Jesus knew he would call out in a loud voice, "Lazarus come forth."

Courageously we ask, "What boulders prevent me from allowing Jesus' words, 'come forth,' to call us from the stink of death?"

Lazarus walked out of his grave. Bound, he was not capable of removing the clothes of death. Mary and Martha, likely standing in shock and awe, needed to be directed to unwrap their alive brother and let him go. Jesus' words "unbind him and let him go" pruned them. I imagine Mary and Martha, years later, mulling over the question, "Why did Jesus need to tell us to take off the grave clothes!"

Do we have trusted people in our lives, those who will listen to Jesus' call to unwrap the clothes of death from us, for us?

A retreat participant asked, "was your divorce pruning?" I paused and thought about pruning in my vineyard. "No, no," I quietly and carefully replied, "pruning took place during my long, painful recovery as God called me to fix my eyes on Jesus only."

Is the death of a loved one pruning? No. The painful journey while grieving the death of a loved one can be equated to pruning. Is illness pruning? No. Treatment, recovery, and redirection of life likely include God's hand pruning as one fixes their eyes on Jesus. Through pruning, the vinedresser welcomes our naked, vulnerable hearts. He works His work, inviting us to fix our eyes on Jesus.

Like all the images I use to unfold our faith life and urge growth, pruning doesn't exactly parallel a particular experience. The disciples in the Upper Room were being pruned as Jesus washed their feet. Mary and Martha were being pruned by Jesus at Lazarus' resurrection. Discerning pruning takes place for a long period of time after it has taken place if one allows themselves to rest in the work of God for them and in them.

At the moment, when pruning takes place, it may feel like pain or confusion. One may feel disoriented or in turmoil. With perspective, distance, and reflection one can see the hand of God at work to sharpen focus on Jesus only. God continues stripping away preconceived notions of who Jesus is as He works in us.

Pruning Questions

Questions uncover a plethora of ways God works to draw us to him. The word of God calls us to meditate on the image of the vinedresser's hand pruning and our hearts submitting to His word at work in us. As we surrender to His hand, we understand more deeply the prime fruit to which we are being called.

God prunes; we receive. We meditate on healing and the sap flowing to the wound created by pruning. God wounds and He heals the wounds He makes. We rest in His work. We are called to seek help if we don't know how to receive or rest in Him.

Processing God's pruning needs movement, growth, and finding one's way after being wounded by the vinedresser, all while resting in Christ. Processing takes time, healing, and a season of rest, from the position of rest *in* Christ, our rest. Not linear in any way, a pruning journey is an odyssey, an adventure, a passage.

Do we unknowingly worship the season of fruit-bearing because we're comfortable there? Pain, confusion, and turmoil go hand in hand with God's work pruning us. Are we susceptible to God's deep work in our hearts and lives? We may be terrified of His work. Do we ignore God's call to rest and be pruned? Do we stay swamped working, unable to pause? God's work taking place is complete *in* Christ, my resting place, and God continues His work in us.

Winter dormancy, the season of deep rest, cannot compare to rapid springtime growth or bearing fruit. The deep wounds created by pruning cannot compare to those made by thinning, just as the season of pruning and the season of thinning differ significantly.

God prunes fruitful shoots of fruitful branches. The pain of the swift cut, the sap, and the healing is the vinedresser's work—a branch can't and doesn't prune its own shoots. As we reflect, we can let out a little chuckle at what a sight we must be to the vinedresser as we scurry around attempting to pick up and glue back on the shoots God prunes.

Questions from God's word stir growth and faith, spurring us forward. Naked and vulnerable before God, questions sink into our hearts. Ponder and embrace these pruning questions as God works through them to position us in Him to bear prime fruit.

Who do you say I am?—Jesus

Jesus asked, "Who do people say that I am?" And they told him, "John the Baptist; and others say, Elijah; and others, one of the prophets." And he asked them, "But who do you say that I am?" Peter answered him, "You are the Christ." And he strictly charged them to tell no one about him. Mark 8:27b-30

Stop, pray, and ponder. Jesus' pruning question is for you, for me. Who is Jesus? How does His work impact our everyday life?

Why did Jesus order the disciples "strictly" to tell no one? Why might our journey of rest and recovery be a period of silence? Maybe we can't comprehend it then, but we see it now, years later. If we talked about meeting up with Jesus in pain, the quiet, the healing, we wouldn't have been able to express the work God was working. Deep pruning cannot be understood until the sap forms a scab, the wound heals, and a visible scar reflects the wound and healing. Healing takes time!

Why do you seek the living among the dead?—The Angel

They found the stone rolled away from the tomb, but when they went in they did not find the body of the Lord Jesus. While they were perplexed about this, behold, two men stood by them in dazzling apparel. And as they were frightened and bowed their faces to the ground, the men said to them, "Why do you seek the living among the dead? He is not here, but has risen. Remember how he told you. Luke 24:2-6a

Stop, pray, and ponder. The angel's pruning question is for you, for me. Why do we seek the living among the dead? Do we seek Jesus through the things of this world that cannot bring life? The *only* place the disciples looked for Jesus was exactly where He told them repeatedly, He would not be. Life cannot be found in deadness. We're called to respond to Jesus' call, "Come forth!"

Do you want to be healed?—Jesus

One man was there who had been an invalid for thirty-eight years. When Jesus saw him lying there and knew that he had already been there a long time, he said to him, "Do you want to be healed?" The sick man answered him, "Sir, I have no one to put me into the pool when the water is stirred up, and while I am going another steps down before me." John 5:5-7

Stop, pray, and ponder. Jesus' pruning question is for you, for me. The lame man did not answer Jesus' simple question. The man stuck pool-side reflected his plight—like we often do. This circumstance, or that, keeps us from receiving Jesus at His word. The water wasn't the thing. Jesus works through water, the word, touch, or a call to come forth. On this day, He worked through the word—that is all. The word is present among us, in us, and we dwell in His life.

Who is he, sir, that I may believe?—The healed man

As long as I am in the world, I am the light of the world." Having said these things, he spit on the ground and made mud with the saliva. Then he anointed the man's eyes with the mud and said to him, "Go, wash in the pool of Siloam" (which means Sent). So he went and washed and came back seeing. Jesus heard that they had cast him out, and having found him he said, "Do you believe in the Son of Man?" He answered, "And who is he, sir, that I may believe in him?" Jesus said to him, "You have seen him, and it is he who is speaking to you." He said, "Lord, I believe," and he worshiped him. John 9:5-7, 36-38

Stop, pray, and ponder. The healed man's pruning question

is for you, for me. Jesus spat and made a mud pie out of the soil. Jesus packed the mud, held together by saliva, onto the blind man's face. Indeed, the blind man couldn't see what Jesus was doing, but those around him did. Most certainly, the blind man could hear the goings on! He received. He washed in the pool, meaning "sent." Jesus sent him away with mud and brought him back seeing, not simply with his eyes. The man saw Jesus with his heart. His heart was hungry to "see" Jesus! "What are we blind to?" We believe and worship Jesus as we see God at work in us.

Do you understand what I have done to you?—Jesus

When he had washed their feet and put on his outer garments and resumed his place, he said to them, "Do you understand what I have done to you? You call me Teacher and Lord, and you are right, for so I am. If I then, your Lord and Teacher, have washed your feet, you also ought to wash one another's feet. For I have given you an example, that you also should do just as I have done to you. Truly, truly, I say to you, a servant is not greater than his master, nor is a messenger greater than the one who sent him. If you know these things, blessed are you if you do them. John 13:12-17

Stop, pray, and ponder. Jesus' pruning question is for you, for me. The upper room symbolizes, most starkly, a place of dormancy and pruning. The confused disciples focused their attention on Jesus, only. The fruit of abiding *in* Christ grows from resting in Christ alone. These verses highlight one aspect of the call—to serve as Jesus served. And there is much more!

Peter's words and actions represent another side of Jesus' call, far more challenging to us than the call to wash the feet of another. Jesus' call is to receive from Him in humility and awe. Many were trained solely in this verse: "It is more blessed to give than to receive" (Acts 20:35). A position of receiving allows us to ask for our deepest need to be met, an intimate connection with Jesus! This pruning question leads us to receive from Jesus that which He came to give—all of Himself.

Trust grows as we visualize the growth falling to the vineyard floor as rich mulch and fertilizer for life. The shoots and buds cut off by the vinedresser could have been fruitful we admit as we tip our toes into the water of the pruning journey. As we gain perspective and look back, we realize God prepared us to bear prime fruit.

Pruning Prayers

Lord, I believe, help my unbelief (Mark 9:24).

Search me, O God, and know my heart (Psalm 139:23).

Your will be done, on earth as it is in heaven (Matthew 6:10b).

Teach me to number my days so that I may gain a heart of wisdom (Psalm 90:12).

Establish my steps (Proverbs 16:9b).

Lead me in your truth and teach me (Psalm 25:5).

CHAPTER III

THE GIFTS

The abundant gifts blessing us in Steinbeck Vineyards include fruit, the harvest, and wine. Another profound gift is the fellowship associated with life in the vineyard. These gifts drive all work in our vineyard, propelling us forward through glorious winter rains, springtime growth and long hot summer days, and bustling fall harvest.

Each gift holds profound insights into life *in* Christ, abiding in the true vine.

Gifts given by our creator invite celebration!

God's word invites us to open our eyes and hearts to these gifts. Through these gifts we see His work in us and through us more clearly.

*May God bless our journey as we
explore His abundant gifts!*

STUDY 12: THE FRUIT

Every year, throughout the year, we work for the fruit of the vine. Fruit is the main thing, and every vineyard practice leading up to achieving mature fruit is fruitful. Our highest goal in our vineyard is prime, ripe fruit for harvest. The shoots unfold, and the fruit forms can be seen. The flowers bloom and pollinate, fruit sets, and then matures.

Every process throughout the year, and, as we've discovered, even the bud growth from the previous year, moves us toward the goal of prime fruit for the harvest. As with our lives, every year in the vine's life is connected to the past and grows into the future. Every fruit-filled word in Scripture connects our lives to the past, present, and future.

Every fruitful word in Scripture connects our lives to the past, in the present, and into the future

The Apostle Paul lived as a branch grafted into the one true vine. The fruit of his pen is as alive today as it was when his letter was delivered to the people of Galatia twenty or so years following Jesus' resurrection and ascension! His profound words call our attention to the fruit of abiding in Christ.

> But the fruit of the Spirit is love, joy, peace, patience, kindness, goodness, faithfulness, gentleness, self-control; against such things there is no law. And those who belong to Christ Jesus have crucified the flesh with its passions and desires. If we live by the Spirit, let us also keep in step with the Spirit. Let us not become

conceited, provoking one another, envying one another. Galatians 5:22-26

Connect Paul's words, "Against such things there is no law," to our trellis system and training discoveries—shoot growth and fruit are not tied to structure but rather grow freely and flourish in freedom. The Spirit of the living God knows no boundaries; we keep in step with the Spirit and are not bound to the structure of the law. We are free to bear the fruit of abiding because Jesus fulfilled the whole law perfectly.

Knowing the tendency to fall into the old way of binding our lives to the law, notice Paul's stern warning, „Let us not become conceited, provoking one another, envying one another" (Galatians 5:26). Recall Paul's words to the people of Rome, "Do not be arrogant toward the branches. If you are, remember it is not you who support the root, but the root that supports you" (Romans 11:18). Paul may have articulated as he spoke, "Do not be arrogant, remember, you do not grow and mature the fruit, God works the fruit of His Spirit in you."

Paul expressed strong words about what is not fruitful in the lives of those grafted into Christ. Note also that discussing bearing the fruit of the flesh draws out the strictest of warnings—eternal separation from the vine.

> I say, walk by the Spirit, and you will not gratify the desires of the flesh. For the desires of the flesh are against the Spirit, and the desires of the Spirit are against the flesh, for these are opposed to each other, to keep you from doing the things you want to do. But if you are led by the Spirit,

you are not under the law. Now the works of the flesh are evident: sexual immorality, impurity, sensuality, idolatry, sorcery, enmity, strife, jealousy, fits of anger, rivalries, dissensions, divisions, envy, drunkenness, orgies, and things like these. I warn you, as I warned you before, that those who do such things will not inherit the kingdom of God. Galatians 5:16-21

"Walk by the Spirit" and "keep in step with the Spirit" provide rich imagery! How else can we live and move when grafted into the life of the vine? As He moves, we move. Remember Paul's words to the people of Athens, "'In him we live and move and have our being'; as even some of your own poets have said, 'For we are indeed his offspring'" (Acts 17:28).

Taste And See

Jump in my Jeep and let's go taste ripe grapes! It is fall, and we've worked all year for this! The bright green shoots of spring and summer wave in the wind less fluidly now. Heavy with a crop, dark green because the energy of the shoots flows toward the maturing fruit, the shoots are visibly stressed. Two clusters of fruit hang from every shoot. The trellis system helps the branches bear the weight of the fruit.

"This fruit is what we work for," I said as I drove my Jeep between two rows. Nose pointed in I stopped at one vine I could reach out and touch from our classroom seat. In one motion, my rusty clippers are slipped off the choke knob, and I snip a cluster of ripe grapes off a shoot, and hand you the beautiful fruit. You pluck a few grapes from the cluster and pop them into your mouth. A wine that tastes great is made from grapes that taste great!

There are three or four seeds in each wine grape. Seeds must be brown to release a nutty flavor into the wine. Mature grape seeds play an important role in the structure and tannins of the wine. Seeds can be chewed, but they will taste bitter.

Grapes release color onto our fingers when we squeeze and roll them between our fingertips. If the color bleeds out, the grape is ripe. If only clear juice rolls down my fingers, the grape is not yet mature. Seed and skin ripeness are essential factors in maturity.

"These are so sweet," you reflect, fascinated by just how many factors go into the ripeness of a grape. Sugar content is critical in a mature grape. We measure the percent of solids using a tool called a refractometer. I open a small gray case and pull out this vital tool. I flip open the glass, squeeze grape juice onto the lens, and close the glass. The liquid spreads evenly over the surface. I put the tool to my eye and looked through the eyepiece. Twenty-three degrees, brix is the sugar quantity.

You take the refractometer and look into the lens and then pass it on, so everyone can see the measurement. We gather large field samples from each block, squish and stir the juice together. We test the whole batch with our refractometer. Twenty-five percent sugar is our goal.

Sugar content, flavor, seed ripeness, and skin ripeness are ripeness factors. Proper acidity is essential too.

We rumble to the top of the ranch and park in the shade of the giant oak tree on the top of Oma's Hill. We rinse our sticky fingers while I silently pray for the words to express more rich connections.

When pondering the fruit of these vines, we don't simply think of this year's crop and the fruit we're tasting right now. We look at the whole picture—six months of field preparation, grafting at the nursery, planting in my soil, training for three years, thinning shoots and fruit, and pruning. These practices are fruitful; our work can be tasted in this fruit right now.

The same is true for our lives! The same is true for Christ's life—His whole life was fruit-filled, toward the primary fruit—being sacrificed as the perfect Lamb of God and rising from the grave.

The Fruit of the Life of The One True Vine

Jesus, Son of God and Son of man, entered time and space through the womb of a virgin.

> In those days a decree went out from Caesar Augustus that all the world should be registered. This was the first registration when Quirinius was governor of Syria. And all went to be registered, each to his own town. And Joseph also went up from Galilee, from the town of Nazareth, to Judea, to the city of David, which is called Bethlehem, because he was of the house and lineage of David, to be registered with Mary, his betrothed, who was with child. And while they were there, the time came for her to give birth. Luke 2:1-6

The Creator became one of us, for us. Jesus' life was formed in Mary's body, born through her body, and nursed at her breasts.

He grew—baby, toddler, young boy, teen boy, young man, and mature man.

Jesus was born in Bethlehem and, to fulfill all prophecy, passed through Egypt en route to Nazareth. Religious leaders cried, "Can anything good come from Nazareth" (John 1:46)? Yes, grace and truth came from God through Mary in Bethlehem, through Egypt, through Nazareth, and Jerusalem. Unwelcome in His hometown, Jesus traveled from place to place, fulfilling God's promises in His holy life.

The Psalmist's words prophetically spoke of the work of the vine. In this Psalm, we see a declaration of God's plan, a cry of brokenness, and the Psalmist begging God to restore the vine He had planted:

> Restore us, O God of hosts; let your face shine, that we may be saved! You brought a vine out of Egypt; you drove out the nations and planted it. You cleared the ground for it; it took deep root and filled the land. The mountains were covered with its shade, the mighty cedars with its branches. It sent out its branches to the sea and its shoots to the River. Why then have you broken down its walls, so that all who pass along the way pluck its fruit? The boar from the forest ravages it, and all that move in the field feed on it. Turn again, O God of hosts! Look down from heaven, and see; have regard for this vine, the stock that your right hand planted, and for the Son whom you made strong for yourself. Psalm 80:7-15

Unlike the unfaithful vine, Israel, Jesus was the true vine

by the Father's blessing and His own testimony. Jesus, the vine brought through Egypt, is depicted here as infinite. The Son, the stock who was made strong, fulfilled all righteousness and every requirement of the law to the letter! The apostle Peter said it this way,

> You were ransomed from the futile ways inherited from your forefathers, not with perishable things such as silver or gold, but with the precious blood of Christ, like that of a lamb without blemish or spot. He was foreknown before the foundation of the world but was made manifest in the last times for the sake of you who through him are believers in God, who raised him from the dead and gave him glory, so that your faith and hope are in God. 1 Peter 1:18-21

Jesus was tempted in every way, yet did not sin (Hebrews 4:15). Jesus healed the sick with touch or a word. Jesus redeemed the leper, an untouchable with a touch, and welcomed a Samaritan woman into His mercy. He raised the dead. The vine spoke truth and light into darkness. He crafted the best wine ever, not of vine grapes, but water. He multiplied bread and fish to feed thousands.

Jesus is the "I am" of all the promises of God. Light, living water, the bread of life, the shepherd, the way, the truth, the life, the door, the resurrection, the true vine. The beginning, the end, the alpha, the omega, the beginning and the end, the root, the bright and morning star. He loved, and He is love. Jesus is all in all for us.

Jesus declared, "Take and eat, this is my body, this is my

blood" (Matthew 26:26). This isn't a likeness; it is the very body and blood of Jesus, the great "I am." Falsely accused of treason and blasphemy against His own Father, Jesus was beaten and crucified with sinners because He was and is the great "I am." Jesus descended into the depths of darkness. For three days, He lay lifeless. God raised His Son to life. Jesus ascended into heaven and is seated on the throne, working for us, and at the same time, He abides in our hearts.

The fruit of Christ's life is finished, and He is still at work at all times. The fruit of Jesus' cry, "Father, forgive them" (Luke 23:34), hits our hearts deeply as we wrestle with the most challenging aspect of life and faith. We acknowledge our need for His forgiveness. We grow and heal in Christ.

"Jesus' Spirit intercedes for us with groans too deep for words" (Romans 8:26-27). Jesus is our home, the life into whom we are grafted. He is our perfection, our righteousness, our healing. Jesus is rest, our rest.

Jesus for us; Jesus IN us; Jesus through us

The complexity of the fruit of the life of Christ places us squarely at His feet, in a position of receiving His work. Jesus watched His Father work, and He worked those works (John 5:20, 36). We live *in* Christ, and *in* Christ's work. We fix our eyes on Him, the author and perfecter of our faith (Hebrews 12:2). From that place, we rest, grow, and bear fruit, the mature fruit of living in His life. Jesus is for us; Jesus lives in us; Jesus works through us.

Fruit of Life *in* Christ

Cabernet vines don't wake up one day and declare that they are going to grow and bear Cabernet fruit. They bear the fruit according to their DNA and from being grafted into a healthy rootstock. The parallel invites awe.

We bear the fruit of being offspring of the one true vine. Jesus is the vine, and we're the branches grafted *into* His life, into a personal, flesh-on-flesh relationship with Him. God's word calls us to be eager to understand the fruit of our lives and grow the fruit of more excellent balance and maturity into the future. Formulas for fruit bearing don't have a place! Working harder? No! The fluid flow of rest, energy, receiving, and growth guides our being! Walking in the works God prepared beforehand for us (Ephesians 2:10) flows from being positioned in Christ. Jesus said,

> You did not choose me, but I chose you and appointed you that you should go and bear fruit and that your fruit should abide, so that whatever you ask the Father in my name, he may give it to you. These things I command you, so that you will love one another. John 15:16-17

We are chosen, appointed, and positioned in Him to bear the fruit of love. In love, we actively pursue that which is best for another. John declared,

> Whatever we ask we receive from him, because we keep his commandments and do what pleases him. And this is his commandment, that we believe in the name of his Son Jesus Christ and love one another, just as he has commanded us. Whoever keeps his commandments abides in

God, and God in him. And by this we know that he abides in us, by the Spirit whom he has given us. 1 John 3:22-24

We bear the fruit of keeping His command to love because we abide in Him and He abides in us. Jesus is love personified and gifts us with everything we need to walk in love. If keeping His command to love originated in us, we could never rest. A fruit of being grafted in Him takes the form of resting in Him.

We implore Jesus to work a deeper faith in us so that we comprehend with our hearts that rest is a place—His body. We beg Jesus to open our hearts and minds to receive Him as our resting place. He calls us into these profound visuals: when we cannot rest or sleep, we're invited to meditate on being held into the vine by a band-aid, sap flowing, healing, and protecting. We can visualize rest *in* Christ because we're grafted *into* Christ at all times. We trust that we are always at rest because we live *in* Christ.

We ask, "Jesus, teach us that your energy flows from our place of rest in you into our lives." The vinedresser brings forth the growth and the fruit of our lives, the very development and fruit He has prepared in advance for us. Excellent fruit is not grown by coercion, pressing for more, or trying harder. The fruit of life flows from our position in Christ, and the vinedresser places the fruit of our lives right in front of us.

The prime fruit to which we are called includes the consistent care of our whole being—body, mind, soul, spirit, heart, and emotions. We care for our being, and from that, flows love and care for others. Many get this backward. They work to bear fruit as they care for others to the exclusion of self-care. These backward attempts create an empty void stemming from a belief that bearing more fruit means being busier. Jesus' call to more fruit and much fruit means prime fruit, flowing from being *in* Christ.

What good works has God placed before you? Make a list. "Husbands and wives, submit one to another out of reverence for Christ" (Ephesians 5:21). Mothers and fathers nurture, teach, and listen to their children. Single? Live whole, lacking nothing, as the bride of Christ. Work? Do your work as though for God Himself. Retired? Student? Grandparent? Pastor? One who listens? Teacher? Learner? We are stewards, caretakers of the work God placed before us that we would walk in it. Rest. Receive. Grow. Produce mature fruit of being *in* Christ, and being precedes doing!

Being precedes doing—simple, not simplistic!

Some of my stories of unrest and immature fruit-bearing may resonate with you, even though they are likely different from your stories. My marriage and my home were not a place of rest. My body and mind never rested. I didn't know how, but I hungered for rest. Jesus' call to me "to ask for anything in His name" frightened me. Giving was safe enough and comfortable; receiving was out of my realm of reality.

Slowly, the fruit of asking and receiving began to grow. I asked God and begged God, day after day, to heal my heart and home. I worked to be better, kinder, more loving, and more beautiful. I pushed myself to get ahead of the fits of rage I knew my spouse would soon throw. "He was kind to others, so something must be wrong with me," I surmised as I bore immature fruit, lacking self-care or self-respect.

My asking gave God only one possibility—to heal my marriage.

Depression and death surrounded me as I worked hard without seeing any fruit of God healing my marriage. God worked a different fruit as I grew, asked, and learned to receive. My spouse's heart was hardened to me and any outside help.

God softened my heart to His work and His word of life. The call to live, heal, and bear mature fruit included the profound visual of sap flowing and healing the wounds on the branches. The tiny shoots and fruit bursting forth in the spring provided hope of a new season.

The image of Jesus as my home and place of rest, sap flowing through my veins just as Christ's blood flows through my body, gave me the desire to live. My weary heart, soul, and spirit slowly woke up to mercy as God worked through those around me for me. These trusted people journeyed with me through my divorce and a long season of pruning and growth.

Shame and fear slowly melted into Christ's wounds as He urged me to rest *in* Him. That place of rest brought and continues to bring forth deep trust and quiet confidence.

Our growth, healing, and fruit-bearing stories are likely quite different; the one true vine is the same yesterday, today, and forever. You may or may not have been a victim of domestic violence,[1]

---

[1] Domestic violence, sexual assault, rape, incest, pornography, alcohol abuse or any type of addiction attacks the very core of one's being, creating confusion, guilt, and shame. Fear and doubt keep even the slightest amount of courage at bay. Women and men caught in the horrible cycle of calm and rage think that no one could possibly believe their story. Help and resources are available in many communities, as are Christian therapists. Unless properly trained, the church and pastors are simply not equipped to truly help one caught in these dangerous positions. Ask for help from God and seek help from those He has placed around you. Healing is a long process. Healing is possible.

but you have most certainly been attacked. Satan wants to victimize those whose lives are in Christ, in any way he can to keep us from bearing the fruit to which we are called.

The apostle Paul makes this statement about the spiritual war with the enemy, "For we do not wrestle against flesh and blood, but against the rulers, against the authorities, against the cosmic powers over this present darkness, against the spiritual forces of evil in the heavenly places" (Ephesians 6:12). Satan attacks specifically in the very place of God's callings in our lives. Paul boldly calls us to put on the whole armor of God (Ephesians 6:10-20) as we bear the fruit of abiding. Grafted *into* Christ's body and armored with God's gear, we are protected by His redeeming love.

Maturing in fruitfulness, we walk forward in the life of Christ. We cling to the fruit of His unending forgiveness, too, as He has finished that work in us and continues to work it. Christ works *through* our stories, brokenness, and pain to heal us. Jesus harvests the fruit of courage to tell our stories as we urge others to trust and quiet confidence in His healing power.

STUDY 13: HARVEST

Excitement builds as harvest season approaches. We pay close attention to many factors, including overall maturity, sugar content, quality, quantity, picking dates, availability of workers, market conditions, et cetera. Knowing we have two to three months of hard work in front of us does not dampen the spirited commotion of staging equipment and readying crews.

Fruit cannot harvest fruit. Like the work of training, thinning, and pruning, each done for and to the vine and branches, grapes must be harvested. The rich Spiritual parallel is that we don't harvest the fruit of our lives.

Contrast that with other aspects of the vines and branches. Left completely untended, grapevines grow fruit. While the fruit quality would not meet winery standards, the vine and branches produce fruit. Sap flows, roots draw in water and nutrients as the plant fulfills the growth function.

The Harvest of the Fruit of Jesus' Life

Jesus' life produced beautiful, mature fruit. Through His life, the righteous demands of the law were fulfilled in Him. He bore the fruit of gentleness and justice, peace and joy. Jesus healed by word and touch; Jesus drew people in and sent people away. He ushered in the kingdom of God in His very life. His suffering, death, and resurrection bore the fruit of redemption. His love defined His being and His actions.

Jesus spoke and worked the work God placed in front of Him. Jesus said, "For the Father loves the Son and shows him all that he himself is doing. And greater works than these will he show him, so that you may marvel" (John 5:20).

Jesus did not harvest the fruit of His life. How and by whom was the fruit of Jesus' life harvested? Jesus' mature fruit was harvested in many ways by those who loved Him. Listeners harvested the fruit of Jesus speaking truth into their hearts. Those who sought Him harvested the fruit of His mercy and love.

Mary and Martha's statement, "Lord, if you had been here our brother would not have died" (John 11:21, 32), reaped the discussion of the resurrection from the dead. Jesus' profound statement followed, "I am the resurrection and the life" (John 11:25). Lazarus' death harvested the miracle of Jesus calling a dead man to life.

Jesus' fruit was harvested in many ways by those who loved Him.

Walking with Jesus through a vineyard harvested the fruit of the declaration, "I am the vine; you are the branches," and the call to abide in Him. Following Jesus on the road adjacent to a barley field harvested the fruit of Him speaking profound parables related to planting seeds or fields being "ripe for harvest." Feasting with Jesus at the wedding of Cana gathered the fruit of Jesus' first miracle, turning water into wine.

Every love story in the Gospels invites us to see the fruit of Jesus' life being harvested.

Jesus' mature fruit was harvested in many ways by those in great need. Blind beggars, the lame, and the mute harvested Jesus' fruit of restoration. The leper harvested the fruit of Jesus' work. He touched one who was deemed untouchable by God's law and healed an outcast.

People in need flocked to Jesus to reap the fruit of mercy and healing! Pause to meditate on Luke's account of Jesus' fruit being harvested from sunset to sunrise in just one day.

> Now when the sun was setting, all those who had any who were sick with various diseases brought them to him, and he laid his hands on every one of them and healed them. And demons also came out of many, crying, "You are the Son of God!" But he rebuked them and would not allow them to speak, because they knew that he was the Christ. And when it was day, he departed and went into a desolate place. And the people sought him and came to him, and would have kept him from leaving them, but he said to them, "I must preach the good news of the kingdom of God to the other towns as well; for I was sent for this purpose." Luke 4:40-43

Jesus' mature fruit was harvested in various ways by those in great need.

The woman at the well's thirst harvested Jesus' "living water" statement and His declaration that He is the Christ for whom she has waited. (John 4) The hunger of the five-thousand harvested the miracle of abundant food and Jesus' words, "I am the bread of life." (John 6:35) Blindness and Jesus healing the man born blind gave sight and an opportunity to worship Jesus. In that same healing act, Jesus, through the healed man, exposed the blindness of the religious leaders. (John 9)

Hate brought forth the rich harvest of fruit from Jesus' life.

Satan's hatred and temptation attempts harvested the mature fruit of Jesus' life. Jesus was tempted in every way, yet without sin. Jesus abjectly rejected and utterly defeated Satan in every way possible. Satan lost. And in and through his hatred and loss, Satan harvested the fruit of fulfillment in Jesus by tempting Him.

Hate-filled, self-serving religious leaders harvested the fruit of discussions of the Sabbath Day as God created it to be. Jesus' proclamation that His very life and body, are our Sabbath rest, was harvested by their hard hearts. Religious leaders attempting to trap or capture Jesus reaped the harvest of Jesus, removing Himself from a crowd because His time had not yet come.

Religious leaders harvested the fruit of the arrest of Jesus, only because Jesus' time had come. Jesus' suffering at the hand of Roman guards yielded the fruit of a life of submission to the work of God through suffering and death.

Many years before Jesus' life, Joseph, the young man sold into slavery by his brothers, declared: "As for you, you meant evil against me, but God meant it for good, to bring it about that many people should be kept alive, as they are today" (Genesis 50:20).

Those who nailed Jesus to the wooden cross harvested the fruit that God had prepared in advance, that Jesus would walk in it. Evil harvested the fruit of Jesus' life. Jesus' torture-filled death yielded the fruit of the sacrifice of the perfect lamb of God. He took the sin of the world, in His body, on that tree. That one day, at the God-ordained hands of those who hated Him, brought forth the fruit of the fulfillment of all Scripture—everything the Old Covenant could not do, God worked in His Son's life.

Mocking Jesus on the cross yielded silence. The guard and the criminal believed. Jesus declared rich fruit to the one hanging next to Him, "Today you will be with me in paradise" (Luke 23:43)! The fruit, "It is finished" (John 19:30), was harvested by hate.

Hate also harvested decisive actions of the Father who had forsaken His own Son for those frightful moments—the earthquake, the darkness, the temple curtain being torn in two, and the resurrection from the grave of countless saints. Those moments included the cry of faith from the heart of the centurion, "Truly this was the Son of God" (Matthew 27:51-54)!

Much mature fruit was harvested through Jesus' preordained crucifixion! The women's fruit of the love reaped a bountiful harvest as grieving women quickly prepared Jesus' body for burial. The donation of the unused tomb by Joseph of Arimathea was harvested in those moments too. The fruit of Jesus' life was sown in tears and reaped with shouts of joy as God's power and energy raised Jesus from the grave (Psalm 126).

Jesus' suffering, death, and resurrection, were harvested by those who hated Him.

The Harvest of The Fruit of The Spirit

The fruit of the Spirit grows in us through our abiding relationship with Christ—grafted into His life. God's call to bear the fruit of the Spirit presupposes a harvest of these fruits. The fruit of the Spirit, "Love, joy, peace, patience, kindness, goodness, faithfulness, gentleness, self-control" (Galatians 5:22-23), are harvested through many means.

How are the fruits of the Spirit harvested? Those who love, those who need, and those who hate, harvest the fruits of the Spirit from our lives. Here are a few examples.

Giving birth to our children harvests the fruit of love, joy, patience, and kindness. Nursing and nourishing them harvest our body's fruit, providing comfort and food. Changing their diapers and bathing them provides examples of self-care. Disciplining consistently harvests the fruit of self-control. Praying at night enriches their faith and ours. Our love is harvested by their love for us and their need for us.

Cooking meals harvest goodness and faithfulness, creativity, and desire for health. Cleaning our homes harvests self-control, stewardship of our belongings, and discipline not to overspend. Working at our jobs harvests leadership, growth, and creativity.

All of the above are examples of the good works God prepared in advance that we would walk in them (Ephesians 2:10). We didn't and don't harvest these good works—God worked the harvest by the little lives, the home, and the work with which He blessed us. Every life circumstance or person in our path harvests fruit.

Branches do not harvest the fruit they bear

We've all experienced the harvest of the fruit of our lives through love and need. God provides many opportunities to develop and harvest fruit borne of trauma and pain. Every life story we've experienced can be viewed through this fruitful lens. Here is one painful example of fruit forming in me at a very early age, maturing in me, and being harvested much later in my life.

My Grandmother endured physical pain most of her adult life. Diagnosed with severe arthritis, she used a wheelchair for the final 25 years of her life. "Sweet and loved by all" describes her well. The harvest of her fruit included popsicles in her freezer for us, homemade meals, and a giant home in which we played.

Even as a child, I could see self-loathing and self-hate deep in her eyes. I could not comprehend it but only felt pain for her. Today I realize shame gripped her soul. I can only surmise the reasons for the hiding and shame from little bits of information shared by the family.

One day I witnessed an argument between my mom and grandfather about my grandmother. As an eight-year-old, I could not possibly understand the argument, but I watched and listened intently. Through tears, my mom attempted to convince my grandfather to get further care for grandma. My grandmother was embarrassed. Her pain and needs were the subjects of such a blow-up, abruptly said, "I'm no good! Just take me out behind the barn and shoot me!"

The argument abruptly ended. I shuddered at the words that had just flowed from the mouth of my beloved grandmother. I don't remember a pause, an embrace, or kind words. I remember the silence and never mentioning the argument ever again. Locked away deep within my beloved grandmother, and in me at a tender age, was the shame of just being alive and having needs.

Years later, the fruit of my love for her was harvested. She lay in a single bed curled up in a 90-pound little ball in the same room of the nursing home in which grandpa died a few years prior. I held grandpa as he died, and now her life's end allowed me to hold her. Frail and in pain, she suffered for a few long days while I stayed at her side. By day I sat in a chair or on her bed. At night I curled up at the foot of her bed and rested to the gurgling noise of her lungs filling with fluid.

Her dying harvested fruit from my heart—the fruit of loving her so profoundly that I refused to allow her to take her last breath alone. And so, she died as I stroked her forehead while sitting next to her on that tiny twin bed.

Over and over, I've pondered and asked, "How many people in our throw-away society feel valueless?" Nursing homes are filled with people that never learned that they have value simply because they *are*. God created them and loved them. They are alive, and they matter merely because they are breathing. They can only receive-a high form of giving as they provide ample opportunity for others to bear the fruit of serving.

I learned from an early age, and these hurting people were likely taught, "It is better to give than to receive." We are a people in crisis because of this single-focus lens! Many believe that because they can no longer give, they no longer have value.

God harvested this truth, that all of us need to ponder: receiving is one of the highest forms of giving!

Fruit formed that day when, as a child, I heard my grandmother's pain-filled words! I've scoured the Scriptures, and I am convinced that the fruit of receiving is one of the most challenging to allow others to harvest from our lives! We're uncomfortable being in a position of need and receiving. In that discomfort, we turn the harvest upside down as we make futile attempts to harvest our fruit of giving.

The word of God harvests the fruit of our lives as we learn to receive from Him and through others. As we receive, faith is harvested from our hearts. God works, also, through our giving, but not solely through giving.

Place your story into the stories of Christ's fruit being harvested through love, need, and evil or hate. Live in Jesus' word and touch on your life story. Beg Him to work His word to grow fruit and bring others to you to harvest the fruit He has produced. Ask these hard questions:

What fruit of your life has been harvested by something the enemy meant for evil? How has God worked through evil and bad for good? What fruit of your life has yet to be harvested from any trauma you've experienced? What has the enemy meant for evil God can and does work through for good?

These are a few examples: The death of a child or a parent, the death of a spouse, illness, depression, the death of a marriage, abuse, rape, incest, an affair, addiction, pornography, genocide, homicide, mass murder, or theft. The enemy meant these for evil; God works through them to bring forth and harvest the fruit of the Spirit.

God continually works through love, through need, and even through evil to bring about the harvest of fruit. Here are a few more examples of the harvest of the fruit of the Spirit.

Love. Our families harvest our love in many ways—our parents, siblings, children, and grandchildren. Working to fight for what is right in our churches and communities and praying for our enemies harvests love amid extreme challenges.

Joy. Laughing and rolling around on the floor with our

children and grandchildren harvests rich joy. Feeling sadness over trauma or tragedy harvests joy. As we journey through the pain of trauma, we begin to realize that joy is harvested many years after the trauma or tragedy.

Peace, kindness, gentleness, faithfulness, self-control. At times this bountiful fruit is harvested through loving people and life experiences apart from suffering. We are called to learn that hurtful life experiences and hate-filled people often harvest the mature fruit of the Spirit through whom God works to bring a bountiful harvest.

The truth that fruit doesn't harvest fruit helps us understand God's work. God works through people, events, and His word to harvest the fruit He calls us to bear.

There are times we need help filtering through the complexities of the harvest! We're called to learn to identify safe people God places in our path, those who help bring forth the mature fruit of harvest in our lives. We need help working through joy-filled times, and we need help understanding the needs of those around us. We also need help interpreting traumatic events, and the hurt people have caused. Those who help harvest the fruit of our lives may include trusted family and friends, pastors, small groups, therapists, or counselors. God sends those people to us to help harvest the fruit of our lives.

Sent to Harvest

Imagine these sights and sounds of Steinbeck Vineyards—40 workers arriving, chatting happily before sunrise. Rapid conversation in Spanish isn't quickly followed, but we understand the smiles and laughter perfectly. These fantastic workers pruned, shoot thinned, and fruit thinned for us. Today they are being sent out to harvest at the vinedresser's direction.

Each worker takes a picking pan from the large stack. The lead worker, the tractor driver, and each team of 8 fire up their John Deere 1070. Workers follow their crew leader and tractor to the designated field just as the rising sun peaks over the horizon.

Clip, drop, clip, drop is the sound of forty workers working quickly—each scooting the picking pan under the next vine and the next with a swift soccer kick. When pans are full, the strongest among them hoist and dump the pans into the large containers on the trailer behind the tractor. Picking pans hold thirty to forty pounds. Each of the two large bins holds a thousand pounds. Pans are thrown or slid, empty back, to team members. So on and so forth, until the allotted amount for the day is picked. Some days they pick ten tons, other days, forty tons. On average, one person picks one ton, 2,000 pounds, of ripe fruit daily.

The vinedresser in Steinbeck Vineyards sends our workers into the harvest to pick ripe fruit. The Spiritual parallels stimulate incredible thoughts. God sent Jesus to bear fruit, fruit harvested by those who loved Him, those who needed Him, those who hated Him, and those who crucified Him. Jesus was sent to harvest the fruit of faith, love, mercy, and a long list of fruit from those who encountered Him. We are sent, too, into a harvest. God sends people into our lives to harvest mature fruit. Harvest is the work of God.

Jesus' words to the woman of Samaria while standing at the well provide a powerful example of a woman harvesting the fruit of Jesus' word and Jesus' word harvesting the fruit of her heart. She knew her need beyond water from the well of Jacob.

Some scholars surmise that this woman was an outcast because she was at the well at noon. I don't see it that way. The Samaritan woman traveled to the well at noon on that day to meet Jesus or more pointedly and profoundly, Jesus traveled to the well that day to meet her. She talked with Him, received Him, and worshiped Him. Meeting Him there harvested this powerful, faith-filled story, the ingathering of the work of Christ.

> *Jesus traveled, at noon on that day, to meet the woman at the well.*

Jesus traveling to meet her flips all attempts to explain circumstances of her call to faith and trust. Ponder these points. First, the whole town listened to her testimony, "Come, see a man who told me all that I ever did. Can this be the Christ" (John 4:29)? Whole towns don't listen to an outcast's proclamation. Second, a Samaritan woman of no stature could not have immediately carried on an educated conversation with Jesus. She told Jesus that she and her people expected a Messiah to come and that He would make lasting connections for them. Ponder the fruit of the woman's conversation with Jesus, harvested by Jesus:

> Jesus said to her, "Woman, believe me, the hour is coming when neither on this mountain nor in Jerusalem will you worship the Father. You worship what you do not know; we worship what we know, for salvation is from the Jews. The hour is coming, and is now here, when the true worshipers will worship the Father in spirit and truth, for

the Father is seeking such people to worship him. God is spirit, and those who worship him must worship in spirit and truth." The woman said to him, "I know that Messiah is coming (he who is called Christ). When he comes, he will tell us all things." Jesus said to her, "I who speak to you am he." John 4:21-26

John recorded these words for us! The harvest of the fruit of the Spirit takes place, as it did in this account, by Jesus meeting us, receiving Him at His word, and worshiping Him for who He is and what He does for us and in us.

Jesus did not send her to harvest the ripe fruit of her people's hearts. She went quickly and willingly with this invitation to her whole town, "Come, see a man who told me all that I ever did. Can this be the Christ" (John 4:29)? The town believed in Jesus because of the woman's testimony.

Jesus stayed with the Samaritans, in their town, for a few more days. Jesus' work harvested their faith. John recorded, "It is no longer because of what you said that we believe, for we have heard for ourselves, and we know that this is indeed the Savior of the world" (John 4:42).

Jesus pointed out to His disciples what the woman at the well already knew and was eagerly carrying out. Jesus spoke these words, "Do you not say, 'There are yet four months, then comes the harvest?' Look, I tell you, lift up your eyes, and see that the fields are white for harvest" (John 4:35).

The believing woman ran to the harvest! Christ's work in her transformed her into a harvester of the fruit of the hearts of eager listeners. Jesus sent 12 changed men into the harvest at one point and 72 at another. "When he saw the crowds, he had compassion for them because they were harassed and helpless, like sheep without a shepherd. Then he said to his disciples, the harvest is plentiful, but the laborers are few; therefore, pray earnestly to the Lord of the harvest to send out laborers into his harvest" (Matthew 9:36-38).

All touched by Jesus are called to be harvesters. All touched by Jesus are also called to submit to the fruit of our lives harvested by those whom God sends to us. The Messiah works this way! Fruit is grown within us, prepared so that we would walk in it. Shoots of branches grow and bear the fruit of abiding. Fruit matures through the hand of the vinedresser, through the vine, and is harvested by those whom God sends to pick the ripe fruit of our lives. The harvest, then, goes into fermentation vats to become the abiding fruit of the vine, the wine.

STUDY 14: THE WINE — THE FERMENTATION PROCESS

Harvested grapes must be processed within a few hours after being picked to achieve high-quality wines. The flurry of the harvest leads to the hustle and bustle of making the wine. Vinedresser and winemaker agree on the picking date and time so that equipment in the wine processing facility is ready when bins of ripe grapes are delivered.

We stop our Jeep next to a full bin of Cabernet Sauvignon grapes and pop a few of the deliciously sweet berries into our mouths. Savoring the flavors leads to imagining the complex flavors of the finished wine three years in the future. We follow the trailer loaded with bins to our winery where the fruit will be processed.

My son-in-law, unloads and weighs each bin and invites us to lend a hand at the sorting table. We exuberantly agree to the sticky job. The fruit is dumped into a hopper and falls through a series of paddles that remove the stems. From there, the fruit falls onto a sorting table where our sorting job ensues.

Everything but the prime fruit gets pulled off the table and thrown into trash bins. We throw away unripe berries, raisins, green stems that make their way onto the table, and mildew-covered grapes. Occasionally we throw out a lizard, a bird nest, or bugs.

A pump hums as it moves the prime fruit into the fermentation vat where natural yeast, living in our processing facility, begins to work. Harvest is complete, our sorting work is finished, and the winemaker's work is just beginning. As the yeast works, heat is created. The winemaker must take the temperature of the wine. Too warm and the fermentation proceeds too quickly. Too cool and the fermentation stalls or stops.

For fourteen to twenty-one days, twice or three times a day, the winemaker performs punch downs. As the yeast works to convert sugar to alcohol, the seeds and skins float to the top and form a cap. As we've explored, skins and seeds are important components in making excellent wine. They must be mixed in a few times a day for the highest quality wine that showcases rich color and tannins.

A unique smell wafts through the air as fermenting grapes become wine. Imagine the smell of bread baking, and you know the aroma of yeast working. Combing that smell memory with very ripe fruit breaking down and your imagination will approach the sweeter bouquet of winemaking.

Fermentation is complete when the yeast consumes all of the sugars in the grapes, converting them to alcohol. This is known as going dry, hence the verbiage, "I enjoy a dry red wine." This dry wine is pumped into a combination of new, year-old, and two-year-old French oak barrels where it ages for two years.

The winemaker checks the young wine and tops the barrels regularly so that outside air doesn't mix with the wine. If that were to happen, the wine would turn into vinegar. He moves the wines from barrel to tank a couple of times during that two-year period to mix the wine together. It's moved back to the barrels for further aging.

Bottling takes place at the optimum time for the wine, a decision made by the winemaker who tastes from the oak barrels regularly. Once bottled, the wine rests for a minimum of one year before presentation and sale to the discerning customer.

The romance of the story of each unique wine vintage captures lovers of wine. No vintage is the same. While this progression happens every year with every varietal we pick for Steinbeck wines, factors we cannot control differ. The vinedresser tends the vines and grows grapes, dealing with the wide variety of factors nature throws our way. Workers pick the ripe fruit, and it's delivered to our winery for processing. Once each fermentation is complete, the wine is placed into barrels and then bottled. Three years later we place the wines in front of our guests. A well-made red wine crafted from premium fruit reaches optimum potential ten or so years after bottling.

The Fermentation of the Wine of Christ's Story

Christ's whole story is the wine of His life. Every step Christ walked, every word He spoke, every miracle, every healing, and every drop of blood He shed completed the demands of a Holy God, His own Father. His three-year journey to the cross, the grave, through the empty tomb, and His ascension is the wine of His perfect life, poured out for you and me.

Imagine every cluster of the fruit of Christ's life in the harvest bin, ready for processing. The grapes are crushed and pumped into a large fermentation tank. As the natural yeast begins to work, heat is created. During the fermentation process, the sugars are consumed by the yeast and converted to alcohol. Rich color, flavor, and tannins are extracted over time—perfectly balanced wine results from the fermentation of the perfect fruit.

The fruit of Christ's life, His abiding fruit, will last. It is preserved for all eternity as the wine of His story. We cherish His words and stories just as we cherish a great bottle of wine, delicious food, and the fellowship we enjoy around the wine. Let's look at some of the stories of the wine of Christ's story.

Jesus' first miracle turned water into the best wine ever made! We've heard the story of the wedding feast time and time again. This time, let's look at it from the perspective of Jesus' whole story as the wine of His life,

> On the third day there was a wedding at Cana in Galilee, and the mother of Jesus was there. Jesus also was invited to the wedding with his disciples. When the wine ran out, the mother of Jesus said to him, "They have no wine." And Jesus said to her, "Woman, what does this have to do with me? My hour has not yet come." His mother said to the servants, "Do whatever he tells you." Now there were six stone water jars there for the Jewish rites of purification, each holding twenty or thirty gallons. Jesus said to the servants, "Fill the jars with water." And they filled them up to the brim.

> And he said to them, "Now draw some out and take it to the master of the feast." So they took it. When the master of the feast tasted the water now become wine, and did not know where it came from (though the servants who had drawn the water knew), the master of the feast called the bridegroom and said to him, "Everyone serves the good wine first, and when people have drunk freely, then the

poor wine. But you have kept the good wine until now." This, the first of his signs, Jesus did at Cana in Galilee, and manifested his glory. And his disciples believed in him. John 2:1-11

Here was the process: Take six empty stone jars and fill them with water. These were jars set apart for the Jewish rite of purification, used for the ceremonial washing of guests before any ceremony. There was no process of growing fruit and harvesting, no crushing or fermenting fruit.

Jesus' wine was made from the fruit of His divine work. Just plain water and Jesus' word made that wine and turned the Old Covenant purification containers into containers of the new wine of Jesus' life. The event host served his good wine first. Jesus made and allowed the host to serve the best wine ever made, by the best winemaker. The master of the feast noticed and pointed it out to the bridegroom. The celebration feast began with good wine and continued with the best wine, through Jesus.

Jesus made the best wine ever, instantly. Making good wine takes three years from start to finish, precisely the number of years of Jesus' earthly ministry. Three years after the miracle of turning water into wine, Jesus spoke to His disciples in the Upper Room. He knew that His steps over the next few brutal hours would crush Him and turn His earthly work into a beverage pleasing to His Father.

For centuries, Jesus' words in the Upper Room instituted the meal that Christians call "The Lord's Supper." During this meal, Jesus used beautiful wine imagery through the words "fruit of the vine" and "poured out for you."

> Now as they were eating, Jesus took bread, and after blessing it broke it and gave it to the disciples, and said, "Take, eat; this is my body." And he took a cup, and when he had given thanks he gave it to them, saying, "Drink of it, all of you, for this is my blood of the covenant, which is poured out for many for the forgiveness of sins." Matthew 26:26-28

Jesus declared, "This *is* my blood, the blood of the covenant, poured out for the forgiveness of sins." Pause and recall our previous discussion, connecting these words to Jesus' "I am" statements. Jesus said, "I am the vine," connecting His life to the fulfillment of God's redemptive word and work. As we discussed, Jesus did not say, "I am like a vine." Jesus would *not* have been hung on the cross had he said, "I am like a good shepherd" or "I am one way of many ways" to the Father.

Jesus did not say, "This wine is like my blood." There would be no need for faith, and there would be no controversy. He declared that through His words and by His power, "This *is* my blood." Through these words, Jesus connected the wine of His life to all of God's demands established in the Old Covenant. In Jesus, the fulfillment of the Old Covenant and ushering in the New Covenant took place. The New Covenant was sealed by His very blood and poured out in this cup of blessing.

Christ's call into fellowship with Him includes feasting on His body and blood through bread and wine. How is this possible? Faith bypasses futile attempts to explain "how" and clings to the truth of the very words of Christ, "this is my body; this is my blood." Faith says, "Amen!"

Cleansing forgiveness flows to every cell in our body through this foretaste of the eternal banquet feast to come. Jesus unites us to His life through His body and blood. Through this meal of rich fellowship, He joins us with one another. Faith declares, "Amen!"

After instituting and serving this holy meal, Jesus made His way to the Garden of Gethsemane. As He and His disciples journeyed, Jesus may have paused in a vineyard (*imagination mine*). In that vineyard, on the way to his arrest, brutal suffering, and the cross, Jesus said,

> I am the true vine, and my Father is the vinedresser. Every branch in me that does not bear fruit he takes away, and every branch that does bear fruit he prunes, that it may bear more fruit. Already you are clean because of the word that I have spoken to you. Abide in me, and I in you. As the branch cannot bear fruit by itself, unless it abides in the vine, neither can you, unless you abide in me. I am the vine; you are the branches. Whoever abides in me and I in him, he it is that bears much fruit, for apart from me you can do nothing. John 15:1-5

Jesus, the great I am, invited, "Abide in me." Jesus, the great I am, declared, "I abide in you." The disciples had just consumed Jesus' body and blood through the Lord's Supper. Jesus' "I in you," through the cup of blessings Jesus had just shared with them was real, even though they couldn't have grasped it in those action-filled moments. The disciples may or may not have immediately recalled Jesus' words in the Upper Room, "Take and drink; this is my blood of the covenant, which is poured out for many for the forgiveness of sins." Jesus was *in* them through the bread and wine, His body and blood.

Jesus is literally in us, too. By His word and His Spirit (John 14:20), His body, and His blood, He lives in us. When we join in the feast of the Lord's Supper, Christians of all times and all places are united as one through the celebration of the lamb of God. This connection we share is beyond words. We receive; we give thanks; we say, "Amen!"

As Jesus walked further down the path toward the cross, He begged God, if it was possible, to remove the "cup" from Him. This cup held the sin of the world and our sin too. The wine of Christ's life included the fruit of the execution of the perfect Lamb of God. By God's will, a brutal execution at the hands of religious leaders claiming to follow God was right in front of Jesus.

> And he took with him Peter and James and John, and began to be greatly distressed and troubled. And he said to them, "My soul is very sorrowful, even to death. Remain here and watch." And going a little farther, he fell on the ground and prayed that, if it were possible, the hour might pass from him. And he said, "Abba, Father, all things are possible for you. Remove this cup from me. Yet not what I will, but what you will." Mark 14:33-36

The wine of Jesus' life, poured out through the "cup of forgiveness" was for all people–religious leaders, the guards, the disciples, you, and me. To those who would humbly receive His work, He granted access as children of God. Jesus' resurrection is ours too. The cup of death could not hold Him. Because He lives in us and we abide in Him, the cup of death through which we must pass cannot hold us.

Fermentation of the Wine of Our Life Story

As with the life of Christ, every bit of fruit from our lives goes into the large fermentation vat and is processed. This imagery helps us understand Jesus' words, "You did not choose me, but I chose you and appointed you that you should go and bear fruit and that your fruit should abide, so that whatever you ask the Father in my name, he may give it to you" (John 15:16).

We abide in Him; the fruit we bear abides. Our fruit lasts! It goes through the fermentation process, a process by which fruit is preserved. The best winemaker ever crafts an elegant product through the fruit of our lives.

Our lives are vastly different from the life of the one true vine and the perfect wine of His life. He is the perfect vine, without spot or blemish. He carried our sin in His body to the cross while never sinning. How, then, can our whole life, all of it, go into the wine of our lives?

We may believe we need to sort out all of the stuff we deem bad, like the fruit passing over the shaking table and workers picking out anything that shouldn't go into the wine. We presume, incorrectly, that only after we sort out the bad stuff will God be able to make wine of the fruit of our lives.[2]

We would be mistaken. We'd be weary, scared, and ashamed

---

2 Please refer back to Study 12 for our discussion of the gift of fruit. Knowingly bearing the fruit of disobedience or hardening our hearts toward God's work that brings repentance and growth to our lives flies in the face of receiving His gifts.

of the bad stuff we'd need to remove to make the wine of our lives. And we would have the process all wrong. We don't make the wine of the fruit of our lives. He does. The master wine-maker works His work.

Jesus redeems our whole story—all of it. He knows every detail! We may focus on the bad stuff as we try to picture God working good wine out of our stories. Pain-filled family experiences and friendships go in. Trauma, emotional and physical injuries, wounds, and scars go in the vat. The pain we've caused others goes in too. Illness and suffering, into the vat they go, along with the mature fruit God has worked in us and through us.

The yeast of His word creates the heat needed for fermentation. By His declaration, like turning water immediately into wine, Jesus places His work over us and in us. The vinedresser grafted us into His Son, the vine and the root. He declares our lives holy, all of it because He is holy.

The wine of Jesus' life was perfect because every cluster of the fruit of His life was perfect. The wine of our lives is excellent, too, because Jesus declares our hearts and lives perfectly redeemed in Him, and He is the master craftsman.

Jesus declares us pleasing and acceptable to God, in Him, right now. The fermenting and wine-making process continues as we live our days on this earth. We've been chosen and appointed by Jesus to bear the lasting fruit of love. We ask the Father to teach us what to ask Him so that our love mirrors His redeeming love.

> You did not choose me, but I chose you and appointed you that you should go and bear fruit and that your fruit

should abide, so that whatever you ask the Father in my name, he may give it to you. These things I command you, so that you will love one another. John 15:16-17

We're confident to beg God for the courage to grow in faith and love. We implore Him to open our eyes to the opportunity to invite people into the abiding relationship with the vinedresser and vine.

STUDY 15: THE WINE — TASTE, SMELL, AND SEE

We've toured the vineyards and participated in the crush, now let's taste our wines! Cabernet grapes in hand, we walk through the front double doors into our rustic tasting room. Pausing to let our eyes adjust to indoor lighting, we take a long look at the decor. The Steinbeck family history is displayed on each wall and the shelves high above our heads, each piece holding a story waiting to be told.

Your eyes are drawn toward the cradle my grandfather and thirty-four Steinbeck children slept in is displayed high above our heads. Beneath it, on the floor below a smart tv scrolling historic and new photos, is a wine press used by our family from the 1880s to about 1950. Your eyes move right to the old forge and then up to the B-26 hanging from the rafters. The story of the 1956 military plane crash on our property takes some time to tell!

The photos capture our attention too. My two favorites are the drip of sap and the grafter's hands. We pause to ponder the richness of the images when coupled with God's word. We move across the room so that I can show you the two impressions of what has become known as "the Jesus vine." One is an untouched photo of a 33-year-old vine in our vineyard, the other is an artist's painting of the same vine. We pause silently, pondering in our own hearts how that one vine grew in Steinbeck Vineyards to reflect so clearly Christ's ultimate sacrifice.

Hearts full, we make our way to the modern tasting bar and rest our elbows on the cool granite. Our senses are stimulated by the sound and smell of wine being poured from bottle to glass. Our nostrils, previously filled with the smell of vineyard dust from our Jeep tour and grapes being processed, now enjoy the aroma of the wine. We look at, smell, and taste the white wine and the rose. Prior to tasting the cabernet, I invite you to taste a ripe cab grape and imagine it as mature wine three years later.

Our senses are stimulated by the sights, the smells, and the tastes we're experiencing. The wine and the stories inspire rich conversation and deepen our connection to one another. God created us, in His image, with multiple senses, so that we can experience Him in a wide variety of ways and through many means. David invited, "Oh, taste and see that the Lord is good! Blessed is the man who takes refuge in him" (Psalm 34:8)!

The Psalmist declared these words as he praises God for the bounty he created, "You cause the grass to grow for the livestock and plants for man to cultivate, that he may bring forth food from the earth and wine to gladden the heart of man, oil to make his face shine and bread to strengthen man's heart" (Psalm 104:15).

Paul called Christ's sacrifice a fragrant offering to God, mirroring the Old Testament language of aromas pleasing God. "Walk in love, as Christ loved us and gave himself up for us, a fragrant offering and sacrifice to God" (Ephesians 5:2).

There are also aromas, sights, and sounds displeasing to God. God cannot tolerate gossip, harsh words, wanting that which is not ours to have, or lust. God hates sin, those committed against Him or against our neighbor.

The heart of God reflects His desire for that which pleases Him. Jesus, only, is pleasing to God. By the redemption Jesus won for us that is ours in Him, the wine of our lives is a pleasing aroma and taste to God.

The Palate of God's Heart

You'll hear the word "palate" consistently in wine culture. The palate includes sight, smell, and taste. When we talk about "your palate," we're referring to your likes and dislikes. What do you prefer, or what are you partial to? We have one rule in our tasting room. Our rule is, if you like it, it is good. We chuckle a bit at this profound truth, and I invite you to be confident in your unique palate.

The palate of God's heart demands perfection. Isaiah knew this fact and shrunk at the thought of the palate of God's heart. When God called him to be a prophet, Isaiah declared, "Woe is me! For I am lost; for I am a man of unclean lips, and I dwell in the midst of a people of unclean lips; for my eyes have seen the King, the Lord of hosts" (Isaiah 6:5)! God knew this fact of Isaiah's existence! God didn't say, "Everything's ok, don't worry. I'll tolerate your lack of perfection and sin because I know you mean well."

God purified Isaiah and declared mercy over him. "Then one of the seraphim flew to me, having in his hand a burning coal that he had taken with tongs from the altar. And he touched my mouth and said: 'Behold, this has touched your lips; your guilt is taken away, and your sin atoned for'" (Isaiah 6:6-7).

Isaiah became a great prophet, proclaiming God's demand for perfect justice and mercy. Amid many warnings, Isaiah spoke to wake up the hard-hearted people. We find this sweet proclamation:

For you have been a stronghold to the poor, a stronghold to the needy in his distress, a shelter from the storm and a shade from the heat; for the breath of the ruthless is like a storm against a wall, like heat in a dry place. You subdue the noise of the foreigners; as heat by the shade of a cloud, so the song of the ruthless is put down. On this mountain, the Lord of hosts will make for all peoples a feast of rich food, well-aged wine, rich food full of marrow, and aged wine well refined.

And he will swallow up on this mountain the covering that is cast over all peoples, the veil that is spread over all nations. He will swallow up death forever; and the Lord God will wipe away tears from all faces, and the reproach of his people he will take away from all the earth, for the Lord has spoken. It will be said on that day, "Behold, this is our God; we have waited for him, that he might save us. This is the Lord; we have waited for him; let us be glad and rejoice in his salvation." Isaiah 25:4-9

the Lord of hosts will make for all peoples a feast of rich food, a feast of well-aged wine, of rich food full of marrow, of aged wine well refined

The palate of God's heart demands perfect wine, a wine that only He can make. He creates the feast too. What are we to do? Do we downplay this demand so our hearts can rest? No, we confess that God cannot tolerate even the slightest stink and is repelled at the taste of anything other than perfection. Christ's perfect sacrifice met God's demand.

God looks at the wine of our lives through Christ's redemption and declares it "good!" Faith says, "Amen!"

Let's review our journey thus far so that you grasp the fullness of this "Amen!" God, the vinedresser, wounded His Son and raised Him to life. The vinedresser grafted us into the life of the vine, the root. He continually works in us to grow fruit in keeping with humility and love. He trains, prunes, and thins.

The vinedresser takes every measure, using all of the senses He masterfully placed in us, to call us into a deeper relationship with Him. The master winemaker crushes and ferments the fruit of our lives.

Just as Jesus miraculously turned ordinary water into the best wine, by His word, He creates the same in and through our lives. We are holy in the life of His Son.

Let's use caution here. Our hearts lean toward, "I'm sort of holy on some of my best days" or "I wasn't so holy today, so I'll try harder tomorrow." God announces, "You are holy and righteous because I have declared it so!" God doesn't say, "you are sort of holy." No! He declares, "You are holy because I have cleansed and purified you in the life of my beloved Son."

What do we do with those not-so-fruit-of-the-Spirit-filled moments of life? What do we do with our lack of love, patience, or kindness? We confess that we have not produced the fruit of love. God, in Christ, forgives. Christ cleanses us through His Spirit and by His very body and blood.

Holiness is not something we do; holy is who we are in Him. Holiness is not something we achieve; holiness is whose we are. We rest in Him. We bear the fruit He grows in us and harvests through the many means previously discussed. Through the heat and purification of the fermentation process, the wine of our lives is a pleasing aroma to our Holy God.

He tastes. He declares our lives fit to join Him at the banquet feast. We rejoice with the David, "You have put more joy in my heart than they have when their grain and wine abound" (Psalm 4:7).

The Heart of the Palate

We taste, smell, and see that wine is good. As our wine palate matures, we have the opportunity to grasp hold of God's desire for the heart of our palate to grow. Freedom in Christ is Paul's desire for us as our love for Him expands. "For freedom Christ has set us free; stand firm therefore, and do not submit again to a yoke of slavery" (Galatians 5:1).

Any and all freedoms in Christ provide the opportunity to praise God through our lives. It is also true that any and all freedoms in Christ provide the opportunity for abuse and misuse. Many fear that if people taste and see that wine is good, they will misuse it. That's a valid fear.

An essential question of the heart is necessary. What have we tasted that tempts our palate away from the fruit of abiding? Are we, like Adam and Eve, drawn toward being the god of our own lives or the ruler over the lives of others? Explore these palates of the heart:

Food is a gift from God to be thoroughly enjoyed. God designed our hunger for food to mirror our deep desire for Him. Some misuse food. Rather than feed their body's need for nutrition, they attempt to feed or starve their deeply buried emotions. Feeding or starving feelings cannot satisfy, and in doing so, they misuse their body. Food is not the problem. The heart is the problem.

Sex is a gift from God to be enjoyed in marriage between husband and wife. Some misuse sex. God's design for intimacy is a gift that draws one closer to their spouse and into a deeper relationship with Him. Rather than honoring God with their body, some misuse and abuse others for their pleasure. Sex is not the problem. The heart is the problem.

Wine is a gift from God to be enjoyed in fellowship, with moderation. God's design for wine is that we would be drawn closer to Him through this beverage. Wine teaches us to taste and see the richness of God's work for us. Wine draws our hearts toward the banquet feast that is to come. God invites us into a deeper connection with Him and with others. Those who use wine to bury physical, spiritual, or emotional pain misuse a gift God deemed good. Wine is not the problem. The heart is the problem.

What do our palates crave? Asked differently, "what do we long for?" When we desire or long for something or someone other than Jesus and the fruit of His Spirit, can we receive Jesus' more profound questions? "Do I want to be healed?" "Why do I seek the living among the dead?" God's working to bring this statement to our weary hearts, "Lord, I believe, help my unbelief."

God designed our palate to mature! Once we taste and see the goodness of God, we crave His goodness in our lives. Once we dine with the master winemaker and master chef, we long for the banquet feast. The heart of God's palate draws our palate into His desire and design. We are one in Him, and we long for His heart. Peter proclaimed,

> So put away all malice and all deceit and hypocrisy and envy and all slander. Like newborn infants, long for the pure spiritual milk, that by it you may grow up into salvation— if indeed you have tasted that the Lord is good. As you come to him, a living stone rejected by men but in the sight of God chosen and precious, you yourselves like living stones are being built up as a spiritual house, to be a holy priesthood, to offer spiritual sacrifices acceptable to God through Jesus Christ. 1 Peter 2:1-5

> You are a chosen race, a royal priesthood, a holy nation, a people for his own possession, that you may proclaim the excellencies of him who called you out of darkness into his marvelous light. Once you were not a people, but now you are God's people; once you had not received mercy, but now you have received mercy. Beloved, I urge you as sojourners and exiles to abstain from the passions of the flesh, which wage war against your soul. 1 Peter 2:9-11

We are chosen and made holy by God. Peter took time to warn that misuse and abuse of all of God's gifts wage war on the soul. We hurt our hearts, souls, and spirits when we go against God's good and gracious will. God longs to forgive and restore. In this same proclamation, Peter quoted Isaiah's words, "He himself bore our sins in his body on the tree, that we might die to sin and live to righteousness. By his wounds you have been healed" (1 Peter 2:24).

Recall that we've connected this rich verse to Jesus' invitation and call to "abide in Him." Healing takes place in the wounds of Christ, now and for all eternity. The palate of our hearts is touched, and all of our senses are engaged. The wine of Jesus' forgiveness and the Spirit of Christ abiding in us moves our spirits to long for more of the heavenly banquet.

Feasting on the heavenly banquet will take place someday and yet, we get a taste of it now as we fellowship around the table with one another. Gather together. Share joys and sorrows. Pray with and for each other. Challenge one another. Read the Scriptures together.

The banquet feast of the Lord's Supper joins heaven and earth through the body and blood of Jesus, through the words of Jesus, and through ordinary bread and wine. As we gather around that festive table, we approach with empty hands and hungry hearts. We have nothing to offer, yet we receive everything—forgiveness, life, and eternal life. We receive the courage to live out our lives, growing in faith and mercy each day. Our palate for sharing Jesus' love with the world matures too.

STUDY 16: THE FELLOWSHIP

As we're enjoying our conversation in our Steinbeck tasting room more guests enter through the double doors. These guests have been here before and gravitate toward their favorite story, guiding their friends to the display of the B-26 crash and the military pieces hanging on the wall. They also point out the "Jesus vine" painting to their friends. These guests have become part of our story, through their engagement with our story.

They enjoy the wines, the stories, and the fellowship. Our team knows their names and greet guests with warm smiles.

On rare occasions, a self-centered guest enters the tasting room. That guest dampens the festive scene by making everything about them. They don't experience Steinbeck; they want everyone to notice and experience them. My team and I flow with the desires of each group of guests. We know a rich, seven-generation story exists, but we don't force that story on our guests.

Jesus knows a rich story exists, but he doesn't force it on anyone. He offers His story. Fellowship or lack thereof is based upon the invitation and the receiving. Those who love Jesus or want to know Him gravitate toward their favorite stories and invite their friends into those stories with them. With eyes and hearts wide open, they receive from the abundance of the word and the work of God.

Like the Steinbeck story, each becomes their story as they walk into Jesus' stories. With eyes and hearts open, those living the experience of fellowship in Christ, proclaim,

> That which was from the beginning, which we have heard, which we have seen with our eyes, which we looked upon and have touched with our hands, concerning the word of life—the life was made manifest, and we have seen it, and testify to it and proclaim to you the eternal life, which was with the Father and was made manifest to us—that which we have seen and heard we proclaim also to you, so that you too may have fellowship with us; and indeed our fellowship is with the Father and with his Son Jesus Christ. 1 John 1:1-3

I remind you of the giant oak tree under which we paused to take in another perspective of beautiful Steinbeck Vineyards. During the tour, our eyes were drawn to a distant view, a picture of the whole. Upon closer look, we notice that the growth of the vines within the circumference of the tree was stunted. The stark reality is that while beautiful and towering above the vineyards, the roots of the giant oak steal the nutrients and water from the vines.

The shoots are visibly stunted, and there are only one or two tiny clusters of fruit. While standing, sipping on a taste of Steinbeck wine, I reflect and ask, "the branches are grafted into the rootstock, but not healthy because of unhealthy competition. What competes with your faith?"

There are persons whose stories revolve around themselves. While the same invitation is offered, a self-centered person, focused only on their own story, may miss the richness of Christ's story and His invitation to grow. Competition from the many ways the world draws us away from fruitfulness in Christ stunts growth as well. Many who are grafted into Christ will be in heaven through His redeeming love, however, they may not have grown the prime fruit of cultivated faith in Christ or live in mature fellowship with others.

Loss of Fellowship Through Betrayal

Judas was a self-centered guest at the table of fellowship during a time when Jesus was suffering greatly. Judas' betrayal began this way, "Then Judas Iscariot, who was one of the twelve, went to the chief priests in order to betray him to them. And when they heard it, they were glad and promised to give him money. And he sought an opportunity to betray him" (Mark 14:10-11). Not long after, in the upper room, Jesus unfolded His knowledge of the impending betrayal,

"Truly, I say to you, one of you will betray me, one who is eating with me." They began to be sorrowful and to say to him one after another, "Is it I?" He said to them, "It is one of the twelve, one who is dipping bread into the dish with me. For the Son of Man goes as it is written of him, but woe to that man by whom the Son of Man is betrayed! It would have been better for that man if he had not been born." Mark 14:18-21

The culmination of the betrayal of Jesus took place through a kiss—a gesture of fellowship. Did Judas truly know what he was doing as he made plans to turn Jesus over to the chief priests? His self-centered nature blinded him to the gravity of the betrayal he was inflicting upon his once friend and teacher. His self-centered actions didn't allow him to see Jesus as one who could save him.

Was Peter one of the disciples who asked, "Is it I, Lord?" Mark recorded, that each and every one of the disciples asked Jesus if they would be the one to betray Him. Moments later in Jesus' passion story,

> Jesus said to them, "You will all fall away, for it is written, 'I will strike the shepherd, and the sheep will be scattered.' But after I am raised up, I will go before you to Galilee." Peter said to him, "Even though they all fall away, I will not." And Jesus said to him, "Truly, I tell you, this very night, before the rooster crows twice, you will deny me three times." But he said emphatically, "If I must die with you, I will not deny you." And they all said the same. Mark 14:27-31

Each disciple asked, "Is it I, Lord?" Mark also recorded that all of the disciples agreed with Peter's lead, saying, "If I must die with you, I will not deny you." They were intent on fellowshipping with Christ, even in His suffering and death.

Judas' intentions were bad; the disciples' intentions were good—simple enough, right? One destroyed fellowship and the others sought, with all of their might, to hold things together, to keep the fellowship. The basic problem of the human heart shines clearly here—all of the disciples were the subject of each question or statement.

Jesus foretold Judas' betrayal and Peter's denial. Jesus fielded all of the disciples asking, "Is it I who will betray you"? He also endured the confident statement of all of the disciples, "If we must die with you, we will never deny you."

Three important verses lay between these two accounts in the Upper Room. Jesus offers the highest form of fellowship with this motley bunch of men—He gives them Himself.

> And as they were eating, he took bread, and after blessing it broke it and gave it to them, and said, "Take; this is my body." And he took a cup, and when he had given thanks he gave it to them, and they all drank of it. And he said to them, "This is my blood of the covenant, which is poured out for many. Mark 14:22-24

He gave Himself, in full fellowship with those who would betray and deny Him. He knew that he would endure brutal suffering and that His death was imminent. He would be sacrificed for their sin and ours. He gave His very body and blood, in fellowship for their forgiveness and a rich connection with them and in them.

Jesus was Lord over their good intentions; Jesus is Lord over our good intentions. Fellowship in Christ doesn't depend upon good intentions or obedience. Fellowship in Christ begins and ends with Him.

Christ's journey to the cross and through the grave was His alone to endure and conquer. There was no fellowship in front of Pilate or while hanging on the cross. His own Father did not fellowship with Him during those dark hours as the perfect lamb of God hung in agony, winning forgiveness for all. The fulfillment of the Scriptures didn't depend on the disciples remaining in fellowship with Jesus. The fulfillment of the Scriptures depended on Jesus and His perfect sacrifice.

Judas couldn't see Jesus as one who could forgive him for his betrayal; the disciples received from Jesus complete forgiveness and peace that passes understanding. We, in humble awe, receive Jesus as Savior. We confess that we would like to be our own savior and that we often believe that fellowship depends upon us and our work. Jesus forgives, restores, renews, and grants us rest in Him. He invites us to the heavenly feast at the banquet table, where rich food and wine abound in fellowship with Him.

Fellowship In Christ

Fellowship statements, spoken by Jesus and recorded by John, bookend John 15. Jesus invites, "Let not your hearts be troubled. Believe in God; believe also in me" (John 14:1). "I have said all these things to you to keep you from falling away" (John 16:1). The disciples' hearts would be troubled by the impending events. The disciples would fall away as Jesus was arrested, convicted, and hung with criminals.

Jesus' words, "Abide in me and I in you," drip of intimate fellowship in Christ. Healing sap, the blood of Christ, binds us together in Him and with one another in royal company. God, the Father, grafted us into His Son's life, and He dwells *in* us. Fellowship and faith are His calls to us and His action for us and in us. Paul said, "God is faithful, by whom you were called into the fellowship of his Son, Jesus Christ our Lord" (1 Corinthians 1:9).

Through baptism, we have been grafted into the vine and the root into His life. Faith in Christ or baptism into Christ is the work of God for us. Fellowship, Paul declared, is solely dependent on God's work in Christ,

> We were buried therefore with him by baptism into death, in order that, just as Christ was raised from the dead by the glory of the Father, we too might walk in newness of life. For if we have been united with him in a death like his, we shall certainly be united with him in a resurrection like his. We know that our old self was crucified with him in order that the body of sin might be brought to nothing, so that we would no longer be enslaved to sin. For one who has died has been set free from sin. If we have died with Christ, we believe we will also live with him. Romans 6:4-8

Thank God that He is the author of our true relationship with Him and fellowship in Him! We abide; He provides all we need for complete rest, growth, and abiding fruit of life *in* Him. We rejoice that Paul's words reflect the Triune God's fellowship with us, "The grace of the Lord Jesus Christ and the love of God and the fellowship of the Holy Spirit be with you all" (2 Corinthians 13:14).

Communion of the Saints

Fellowship in Christ exponentially exceeds our human understanding. John uses these words to call us into a deeper understanding of the fellowship of the Son to the Father and the Son to us, "In that day you will know that I am in my Father, and you in me, and I in you" (John 14:20). Christ's declaration instigates and secures an abiding, fellowship relationship by His doing—incomprehensible and graspable only by faith.

The Passover meal connected the children of Israel in

fellowship as they prepared to flee the bondage of Pharaoh. They painted the blood of an unblemished lamb on their doorposts. The Passover meal they shared bound them to the work of God, protecting them from the angel of death. Death passed over the homes on which the blood was painted. In the Passover meal, celebrated by Christians through the centuries as the Seder Meal, fathers declared to their families, "once we were slaves to Pharaoh in Egypt, but the Lord in His goodness and mercy redeemed us from that land with a mighty hand and an outstretched arm" (Deuteronomy 5:15).

Redemption with outstretched arms took place as Christ, the perfect lamb of God, took our place and received the punishment we deserved. The Lord's Supper, instituted by Christ in the upper room just before his betrayal, grants us fellowship with Him and with every believer of all time. The angel of death did not pass over Christ because He submitted Himself to death. The angel of death passes over us through Christ's perfect and ultimate sacrifice, foreshadowed in the Passover events.

Jesus, the lamb of God, declared, "Whoever would be great among you must be your servant, and whoever would be first among you must be your slave, even as the Son of Man came not to be served but to serve, and to give his life as a ransom for many" (Matthew 20:26b-28). Jesus is the host, the one who serves. Jesus' body and blood, given and shed for us for forgiveness, is the meal.

> *Jesus is the host. Jesus is the one who serves. Jesus is the meal.*

We receive from Him forgiveness, life, and salvation. Our fellowship with Him and in Him, is not dependent on our intentions or strength. We rejoice that our fellowship with one another depends on His word and work. Love is the identifying mark of fellowship with Him and with one another.

The fruit of the Spirit exudes forth from us by the power of the Holy Spirit. He teaches, He guides, and He brings to our minds the words and work of Christ for us and in us. The Spirit of the living God binds us together in fellowship in Him and with one another now and for all eternity.

CHAPTER IV

THE VINEDRESSER'S CALL

The vinedresser's call urges us into these concluding connections—terroir, balance, connecting, abiding, and the multiplication of the Gospel.

Terroir is a French word meaning "a sense of place." Merriam-Webster's Dictionary defines terroir as "the combination of factors including soil, climate, and sunlight that gives wine grapes their distinctive character." We will further explore Jesus as our home, our abiding place.

Balance bursts forth as critical life, vine, and wine images. As with human beings, vines and wines require care to maintain balance. Vinedressers and winemakers work tirelessly balancing and identifying, and fixing imbalances.

Vines and branches, coupled with the powerful word of God, invite us further into the beauty of the concepts of connecting and abiding. Abiding in the vine, joined to Him by the work of the vinedresser, produces faith, hope, and love. He connects us, too, with one another, through Christ, the true vine.

Finally, we'll dive into the multiplying nature of growth. The Gospel of Jesus Christ works exponentially, just as one vine multiplies the crop or a little yeast multiplies in a vat of juice to ferment grapes into wine.

STUDY 17: TERROIR

Terroir (ter'wär) is a French word Merriam-Webster defines as "the combination of factors including soil, climate, and sunlight that gives wine grapes their distinctive character." It is commonly summarized as a sense of place. The taste of grapes is unique to the region of the world in which they are grown. For example, grapes grown in Paso Robles are distinctively different from those in Napa Valley, even when viticulture practices are of equal quality. Wines are distinct too.

Paso Robles is located exactly halfway between San Francisco and Los Angeles. California's beautiful Central Coast, less than an hour's drive, includes Morro Bay, Pismo Beach, Avila Beach, and Cambria. The famous Hearst Castle is located in San Simeon. The Coastal Mountain Range separates us from the beaches and creates an entirely different climate than at the coast. Morro Bay might be 55 degrees on an August day. Paso Robles, on that same day could be 105 degrees!

Paso Robles averages a 40-degree temperature swing during the grape growing season. Hot days and cool nights are markers of our particular area of the world, making our grape-growing and wine-making unique. That uniqueness is distinct enough that highly sensitive and well-trained palates can distinguish wines from Paso Robles and those grown and made anywhere else in the world.

A person trained and certified by the Court of Master Sommeliers, as a Master Sommelier, must be able to recognize those differences. By smell alone, these well-trained individuals can name the terroir in which the grapes were grown, and the wine originated. To be certified, they are also required to identify the year the wine was produced—from regions around the world. As if that weren't enough, whiskeys and beers from around the world must be identified too. As of this writing, the Court of Master Sommeliers indicates 273 Master Sommeliers worldwide have earned this prestigious honor.

A Place, A Time, A Person

Christianity has a recognizable, distinctive terroir in the person of Jesus. Jesus was born in a specific place at a particular time in history. The Scripture declares that He was born in Bethlehem, in a manger, when Quirinius was governor of Syria (Luke 2:2). Shepherds helped welcome Jesus into the world.

Wise men traveled to Bethlehem from the East, following a star to Bethlehem, to worship Jesus because of these words from the prophet Micah, "But you, O Bethlehem Ephrathah, who are too little to be among the clans of Judah, from you shall come forth for me one who is to be ruler in Israel, whose coming forth is from of old, from ancient days" (Micah 5:2).

Mary and Joseph fled to Egypt to avoid Herod's decree to kill the one who would rule over him to fulfill Hosea's prophecy. "When Israel was a child, I loved him, and out of Egypt I called my Son" (Hosea 11:1). Mary, Joseph, and Jesus' journey brought them out of Egypt into Nazareth. Matthew recorded,

> When Herod died, behold, an angel of the Lord appeared in a dream to Joseph in Egypt, saying, "Rise, take the child and his mother and go to the land of Israel, for those who

sought the child's life are dead." And he rose and took the child and his mother and went to the land of Israel. But when he heard that Archelaus was reigning over Judea in place of his father Herod, he was afraid to go there, and being warned in a dream he withdrew to the district of Galilee. And he went and lived in a city called Nazareth, so that what was spoken by the prophets might be fulfilled, that he would be called a Nazarene. Matthew 19:19-23

John begins his Gospel with creation—in time, God spoke and created, through the word, the man Jesus Christ. He proclaimed, "And the Word became flesh and dwelt among us, and we have seen his glory, glory as of the only Son from the Father, full of grace and truth" (John 1:14). John moves from the vastness of the world created by the word to the man Jesus, born in time and place. He recorded John the Baptist's baptism of Jesus and then through the phrase "the next day," indicated three additional days following Jesus' baptism (John 1:29, 35, 43).

Jesus' baptism, the calling of the disciples, Jesus' miracles, and all of His life events took place in time and specific places. Paul proclaimed, "But when the fullness of time had come, God sent forth his Son, born of woman, born under the law, to redeem those who were under the law, so that we might receive adoption as sons" (Galatians 4:4-5). John recorded Nathanael's question, "Can anything good come out of Nazareth?"

The next day Jesus decided to go to Galilee. He found Philip and said to him, "Follow me." Now Philip was from Bethsaida, the city of Andrew and Peter. Philip found

Nathanael and said to him, "We have found him of whom Moses in the Law and also the prophets wrote, Jesus of Nazareth, the son of Joseph." Nathanael said to him, "Can anything good come out of Nazareth?" Philip said to him, "Come and see." John 1:43-46

Nathanael knew terroir—a sense of place, the land. We know terroir. We, too, live in a specific place at a particular time. Jesus has called us and redeemed us, here, now, where we are.

Terroir In Christ

The vinedresser's plan of redemption in Christ took the form of a promise to Adam and Eve. They disobeyed a holy God. Sin entered the world through them, in a specific place, in the Garden of Eden. God's righteous punishment included kicking them out of the perfect Garden and into an unfamiliar terroir where they would know weeds, pain, and death.

The vinedresser made a promise, and God placed himself in history at a time and place through that promise. His Son, the word made flesh, took center stage. Every promise God made was rooted in His covenant with His people. The Psalmist declared,

> He is the Lord our God; his judgments are in all the earth. He remembers his covenant forever, the word that he commanded, for a thousand generations, the covenant that he made with Abraham, his sworn promise to Isaac, which he confirmed to Jacob as a statute, to Israel as an everlasting covenant, saying, "To you I will give the land of Canaan as your portion for an inheritance." Psalm 105:7-11

For a time, the focal point of God's covenant was the land. Or was it? God's redemption plan always focused on God and life through His son! "He saved them" is spoken repeatedly in the Scriptures because God must be faithful to His promises. "Yet he saved them for his name's sake, that he might make known his mighty power" (Psalm 106:8). The focal point of God's salvation history has always been the person, Jesus Christ.

We are grafted into the terroir God intended for us and all people—Christ's holy life. He walked this earth, born of Mary. He was God in skin. He is eternal. Reflect on Paul's words from the perspective of being grafted into Christ, our home, our perfect terroir.

> In him we have redemption through his blood, the forgiveness of our trespasses, according to the riches of his grace, which he lavished upon us, in all wisdom and insight making known to us the mystery of his will, according to his purpose, which he set forth in Christ as a plan for the fullness of time, to unite all things in him, things in heaven and things on earth. Ephesians 1:7-10

> But when the fullness of time had come, God sent forth his Son, born of woman, born under the law, to redeem those who were under the law, so that we might receive adoption as sons. And because you are sons, God has sent the Spirit of his Son into our hearts, crying, "Abba! Father!" So you are no longer a slave, but a son, and if a son, then an heir through God. Galatians 4:4-7

> Therefore, as you received Christ Jesus the Lord, so walk in him, rooted and built up in him and established in the faith, just as you were taught, abounding in thanksgiving. In him also you were circumcised with a circumcision made without hands, by putting off the body of the flesh, by the circumcision of Christ, having been buried with him in baptism, in which you were also raised with him through faith in the powerful working of God, who raised him from the dead. And you, who were dead in your trespasses and the uncircumcision of your flesh, God made alive together with him, having forgiven us all our trespasses, by canceling the record of debt that stood against us with its legal demands. This he set aside, nailing it to the cross. Colossians 2:6-7,11-14

Paul calls us to an eternal perspective, a faith based on God's salvation history into which we are placed by the vinedresser's hand. Eternity is now *in* Christ, our abiding place. Eternity face to face *in* Christ is our future. Eternity in Christ includes all of God's salvation history in the past. Past, present, and future *in* Christ are the holy terroir in which we abide.

Jesus declared to the Jewish leaders, "Truly, truly, I say to you, before Abraham was, I am" (John 8:58). In this statement, Jesus bound Himself to God's covenant to Moses, who was instructed to declare, "I am sent me" (Exodus 3:14b). When Jesus declared, "I am the true vine, and my Father is the vinedresser" He bound Himself to God's work through Moses. When Jesus invited us to abide in Him, He revealed one more aspect of Himself as the great "I am." In baptism and through faith, having been grafted into the eternal, holy life of Jesus, we abide *in* the life, the terroir of the great "I am."

By all outward appearances, we are bound by the land and by time. We live in a particular place. We were born at a particular time in a particular place—that is part of our life story. You may choose to travel here, to Steinbeck Vineyards, and I hope you do. Regardless, "Immanuel, God with us," is with us and in us. We are bound together in Him. Like a Master Sommelier, Jesus the master of all masters has called us by name. He knows our home because it is His very life. The terroir in which we live grounds us for an even broader life story, in the eternal life of the one true vine.

I spoke this rich truth at a women's retreat. A dear lady approached me after the session and said, "my husband is in the military. We receive orders to move every two years. I am so tired of moving! I'm exhausted!" She continued, "you helped me understand that my home is *in* Christ and that I'm changing houses but not changing my home."

Two years later, I spoke again to this group. She approached me and with sad eyes, said, "It's happening again. We have to move. I didn't want to come today to hear you speak, because I knew you'd talk about being grafted into Christ, our home. I'm here because I need to hear it again so that God softens my heart to moving, to changing communities, making new friends, and moving to a new house."

The message of Christ as our eternal terroir touches our hearts and makes a real difference in our day-to-day life. Knowing that our home on this earth is temporary and that our home in Christ is eternal gives us pause to reflect on being rooted and grounded in Christ. Christ as our home stirs our hearts to invite others into our beautiful, eternal home.

STUDY 18: BALANCE

When you visit little Paso Robles, you will see that we have grown up as a premier wine region in California. A charming combination of old and new welcomes guests from around the globe. Guests can tour the historic ballroom of the Paso Robles Inn on their way to the Piccolo Hotel, complete with a rooftop bar that overlooks the city—the Inn was completed in 1889, and the new hotel in 2019. Our new city library sits opposite the historic Carnegie Library.

You'll find a balance of old and new in Steinbeck Vineyards, too. Giant old cabernet vines (1982) on one side of my driveway and baby cabernet on the other. My modern wine processing facility sits a stone's throw from my home, built in 1921. A shiny new machine harvester rests in the shade of an old barn. Our 1958 Willys Jeep parks next to new vehicles. "Rustic elegance" accurately describes my wine-tasting room as modern track lighting illuminates old family treasures.

Balance surrounds us as we tour my vineyards. The soil, canopy, and fruit need balance. The focus of the vinedresser and winemaker requires a constant focus on balance. High nitrogen levels in the soil mean the fruit cannot ferment properly during winemaking. Too little shoot growth leads to a carbohydrate deficiency—the fruit cannot mature without fuel. Wine flavors are impacted if there is excessive shoot growth. Rainfall extremes affect the vines too. Excess fruit weakens the vines for the following year. Our wine feels flat on the palate if acids and flavors are not balanced.

Balance is critical! When an imbalance problem stumps our vinedresser or winemaker, who have over 100 years of combined experience, they ask for expert advice. This is an often overlooked important detail as we explore the images of vines and wine.

God's word invites us to acknowledge that we are created with the need for outside help to maintain balance. We need God's instruction through His word to balance our lives. We need faithful, wise people around us to observe, guide, and instruct us. We need authentic, genuine people to lovingly call out areas of imbalance. When we try to achieve balance in a vacuum, we create even more complex and often hidden layers of imbalance.

When we try to achieve balance in a vacuum, we create layers of imbalance

Life's Balance—God's Design

God spoke balance into being—the sun, moon, earth, and stars. Day. Night. Seasons. He's the expert! God kept and keeps balance in place through His mighty work. Even on the seventh day, when Scripture tells us God rested, He still worked to sustain the creation He had created. While God rested He worked.

God created Adam by scooping up a pile of dust and shaped Adam's body in perfect balance and breathed into Him the breath of life. Dust scatters when I breathe on it or blow into it. The breath of God into the dust brought Adam to life. "Then the Lord God formed man of dust from the ground, and breathed into his nostrils the breath of life; and man became a living being" (Genesis 2:7 NASB).

Through the breath of God, Adam became a "living being." These two powerful words envelop God's creative design for balance.

The concept of "being," must be grasped in the context of the Eastern world. "Being" encompasses the whole being—body, soul, spirit, heart, mind, emotions, and senses. Anything short of that misses God's excellent, masterfully creative design flowing from His breath. Adam and Eve were entirely and fully balanced, living human beings, by God's design and breath.

Sadly, on this earth, we will never know the balance Adam and Eve enjoyed in the Garden of Eden. They disobeyed God, and their disobedience is our inheritance. God has much more for us than a resignation to a life of imbalance. Think back to the images presented throughout our study. We're grafted into Jesus, the vine and the root. The healing sap flow mirrors Christ's cleansing blood flowing through us. Now add the concept of the breath of God breathing life, creating balance.

The breath of God breathes life into our being, our whole being! We inherited imbalance. God breathes, and through His breath, He creates aliveness in us. Paraphrasing Genesis 2:7, we can confidently say, "And we become 'living beings' through His breath." Paul invites us into his "inner being," "whole being," language,

> For this reason I bow my knees before the Father, from whom every family in heaven and on earth is named, that according to the riches of his glory he may grant you to be strengthened with power through his Spirit in your inner being, so that Christ may dwell in your hearts through

faith—that you, being rooted and grounded in love, may have strength to comprehend with all the saints what is the breadth and length and height and depth, and to know the love of Christ that surpasses knowledge, that you may be filled with all the fullness of God. Ephesians 3:14-19

In addition to inheriting imbalance from Adam and Eve, our life experiences have contributed to imbalance. How were we nurtured? Was it with gentleness and consistency? Was it balanced? Our roots matter in the things and ways of God! He redeems, heals, and restores. He nurtures with gentleness and consistency.

Ponder balance and imbalance in human beings while drawing rich imagery from vineyard and wine balance. The overall health of the vine and quality of the fruit and wine can be traced back to the origins of the little vine—was it healthy and well cared for so that it produces fruit from balance?

Our whole-being balance can be traced to the earliest experiences in our families. Pause in Paul's tender words, "We were gentle among you, like a nursing mother taking care of her own children. So, being affectionately desirous of you, we were ready to share with you not only the gospel of God but also our own selves, because you had become very dear to us" (1 Thessalonians 2:7-8).

One of the first experiences newborn infants encounter occurs at their mother's breasts. Think of the image of God-created balance. The newborn connects with his mother taking in food while experiencing deep connection and balance. This important relationship provides connection and balance first, food is secondary. Food flows from connection and balance. The same is true for the growing child. Skin contact continues, and now the baby gazes into his mother's eyes while nursing, first one breast, then the other.

There are times a mother cannot nurse. Balance and bonding can still occur through skin contact, closeness, eye-to-eye contact, and switching sides when bottle feeding. This is a necessary component of growth and development, a significant stepping stone to a child being able to function as a whole, balanced being later in life. God-designed balance takes place from life's first breath and continues in frequent, precious moments between caregiver and child.

The earliest connections in our families carry weight as it relates to our relationship with God. Do we feel close to Him? Are we connected to Him? Balanced in Him? Fed by Him? Again, make the connections through the images of grafting, vineyard and wine balance, training, thinning, and pruning! God created us for connection and balance. He breathes into us, recreating in us what His desire is for us.

> ***God breathes His breath into us, recreating in us that which is His desire for us***

As the child develops, parents and caregivers teach and train. Self-control is a fruit of the Spirit, harvested by those placed by God to care for the child. Self-care—body, soul, heart, mind, spirit, emotions—must be taught and harvested. God's gracious, holy design provided the family unit to train a child—self-control, self-care, and eventually other-care. Once grown, an individual is responsible for self-control and self-care. Flowing out of self-control and self-care is the ability to care for others in balanced, healthy ways.

Our whole being, as God designed needs careful attention and intentional care. Self-care is not selfish, as some have judged. Self-care is a high and holy calling from God to each of us. We are stewards of His gift of life, our life.

Our complex being is a gift from God, a gift we cherish and take full responsibility for. We declare with David, "For you formed my inward parts; you knitted me together in my mother's womb. I praise you, for I am fearfully and wonderfully made. Wonderful are your works; my soul knows it very well" (Psalm 139:13-14). The following are examples to ponder as we reflect on balance in our lives.

BODY-CARE: Scripture calls us to body care. Seemingly simple, personal hygiene, a daily routine of caring for the body God gave us, is one of the many good works that God prepared in advance for us to live out (Ephesians 2:10). Exercise and rest, eating healthy food, gazing upon beauty with our eyes, and touching beauty with our hands are aspects of balance—simply breathing and reflecting on the breath of God breathing life into our body.

SOUL-CARE: Scripture calls us to soul care: "Only take care, and keep your soul diligently, lest you forget the things that your eyes have seen, and lest they depart from your heart all the days of your life" (Deuteronomy 4:9). How do we care for our soul? We feed our soul with the word of God and surround our lives with those who will speak God's word, soul words, to us! "Gracious words are like a honeycomb, sweetness to the soul and health to the body" (Proverbs 16:24). David despaired as he hid in the cave: "Look to the right and see: there is none who takes notice of me; no refuge remains to me; no one cares for my soul" (Psalm 142:4). We are called to place ourselves into proximity to those who will care deeply for our soul.

HEART-CARE: Scripture calls us to heart care. How do we care for our hearts? We receive Christ's work cleansing and making our heart whole. We cherish His life alive in our hearts. "When the cares of my heart are many, your consolations cheer my soul" (Psalm 94:19). We seek mature individuals to journey with us. "The purpose in a man's heart is like deep water, but a man of understanding will draw it out" (Proverbs 20:5). „Keep your heart with all vigilance, for from it flow the springs of life" (Proverbs 4:23). We are called to place ourselves into proximity to those who will care for our hearts.

SPIRIT-CARE: Scripture calls us to spirit care. How do we care for our spirit? Christian music feeds my spirit. The word of God feeds my spirit. Worship with brothers and sisters in Christ feeds my soul and spirit. Solomon shared this heart's wisdom. "A glad heart makes a cheerful face, but by sorrow of heart the spirit is crushed" (Proverbs 15:13). „A joyful heart is good medicine, but a crushed spirit dries up the bones" (Proverbs 17:22). „The spirit of man is the lamp of the Lord, searching all his innermost parts" (Proverbs 20:27). We are called to place ourselves into proximity to those who will care for our spirits.

EMOTION-CARE: Scripture calls us to emotional care. How do we care for our emotions? One way is to acknowledge that, like our body and soul, God created emotions and feelings to be an integral part of our being. Meditate on these verses: "You have turned for me my mourning into dancing; you have loosed my sackcloth and clothed me with gladness" (Psalm 30:11). "For our heart is glad in him, because we trust in his holy name. Let your steadfast love, O Lord, be upon us, even as we hope in you" (Psalm 33:21-22). "Jesus wept" (Luke 11:35). "Looking to Jesus, the founder and perfecter of our faith, who for the joy that was set before him endured the cross, despising the shame, and is seated at the right hand of the throne of God" (Hebrews 12:2). "These things I have spoken to you, that my joy may be in you, and that your joy may be full" (John 15:11). "Be angry and do not sin; do not let the sun go down on your anger" (Ephesians 4:26).

Out of Balance

Balance integrates one's whole being; imbalance leads to disintegration—balance ushers in calm and ease; imbalance—dis-ease. Lack of attention and improper care takes a toll on the overall balance in life. For example, if parents feed a child food three times a day but don't provide training in self-care, the child will be out of balance. Imbalance also takes place when emotions are denied. The other extreme is true: imbalance occurs when life is lived only in emotion and not common sense and mindfulness. A child grows up out of balance when their spirit, soul, and heart are not fed.

Shame runs rampant as immature adults raise children. Immaturity and imbalance flow freely from those who were not taught soul, spirit, heart, and emotional care. Ponder these common shaming statements: "Children are to be seen, not heard." "Anger is wrong." "You have nothing to be afraid of." "Quit your crying, or I'll give you something to cry about." Children learn to be invisible, swallow anger or fear, and stop crying or attempting to express their God-designed needs. This, of course, leads to varying levels of disconnection.

Disconnection wages war on one's soul! Disconnection leads to unhealthy activities that further wage war on the soul. Reflect again on Peter's words, "Beloved, I urge you as sojourners and exiles to abstain from the passions of the flesh, which wage war against your soul" (1 Peter 2:11).

Not all individuals experience trauma, but for those who have, care is necessary to achieve a healthy balance. Trauma takes many forms, and each deals with trauma differently. One thing is certain—profoundly distressing or disturbing traumatic experiences lead to imbalance. Trauma adds to shame-based behaviors of many forms.

Trauma leads to loneliness, anxiety, anger, sadness, tension, a racing mind, and physical illness. Trauma also leads to exhaustion, confusion, agitation, numbness, and dissociation. Trauma equals loss. Loss takes many forms. It may mean loss of trust, hope, joy, creativity, imagination, and energy.

Many children and young adults experience trauma and upset at the very hands of people called to care for and nurture them. We see far too much abuse, incest, rape, and pornography. The list includes but is not limited to sex trafficking, murder, and mass bombings or shootings. We see war and its traumatic effects on people. Natural disasters like fires, earthquakes, floods, hurricanes, and tornadoes create trauma.

Each individual is responsible for self-care so that the effects of trauma can be dealt with in healthy ways. Healthy enough adults nurture children and young adults to grow up in every aspect of their complex being. Guiding and directing, making room for needs and fears, and correctly identifying God-given emotions play a significant role in child development and maturity. When trauma occurs, patient parents encourage processing. Healthy enough parents know when to ask for the help of trained professionals equipped to help bring balance from imbalance.

Trauma happens. Grieving trauma, perhaps not so much! Many, many people don't know what grieving looks and feels like. Many do not permit themselves to grieve. Many grieve inwardly in shame. Far too many live out destructive, imbalanced, and disconnected behaviors.

We learn from vines and branches and from our bodies when wounded. Sap and blood flow out. Cuts on our skin bleed outward to cleanse the wound and begin the process of healing. We need safety to be balanced and connected! We need protection in the word of God, and we need safe people with whom to process the pain of wounds.

Safe people provide a safe place to express our emotions and cry out in pain from the wounds of our hearts, soul, and spirit. An out-of-balance David begs God for help, for balance through these words:

Be merciful to me, O God, be merciful to me, for in you my

soul takes refuge; in the shadow of your wings I will take refuge, till the storms of destruction pass by. I cry out to God Most High, to God who fulfills his purpose for me. Psalm 57:1-2

Save me, O God! For the waters have come up to my neck. I sink in deep mire, where there is no foothold; I have come into deep waters, and the flood sweeps over me. I am weary with my crying out; my throat is parched. My eyes grow dim with waiting for my God. Psalm 69:1-3

With my voice I cry out to the Lord; with my voice I plead for mercy to the Lord. I pour out my complaint before him; I tell my trouble before him. Psalm 142:1-2

With my voice I plead for mercy to the Lord

Breathe, Ask

Likewise, the Spirit helps us in our weakness. For we do not know what to pray for as we ought, but the Spirit himself intercedes for us with groanings too deep for words. And he who searches hearts knows what is the mind of the Spirit, because the Spirit intercedes for the saints according to the will of God. And we know that for those who love God all things work together for good, for those who are called according to his purpose. Romans 8:26-28

Breathe and ask: "Does our *being* define our *doing*?" Or "Does our *doing* define our *being*?" Ask more. "Are we of value to God simply because we are a living, breathing human being?" Do we believe that once we can no longer accomplish any work, are we valuable?

A newborn baby and a dying person in a nursing home have this in common—value and vulnerability. Their value is simply in being. They are vulnerable and at the mercy of the hands and hearts of those serving them. They receive. A newborn knows nothing more. They express needs; they receive; they rest.

The individual in the nursing home may have been a strong and capable giver their entire adult life. Embarrassed at being needy and horrified at being vulnerable, they war within and without. No longer able to do and never having learned to be, they despair of life itself. What are the good works of this individual? Receive. Rest. Say, "Thank you."

Shame, trauma, stress, inward grieving, and any other imbalanced way of being drive fear of the answer to these questions. Fear drives us to more work, more doing. It's time to lean into our fears and run to God's word. God's word declares our being valuable. Our head knows this fact. Has that knowledge permeated our hearts, soul, and spirit? Is our being balanced?

Why is leaning into pain hard? Why is receiving challenging? We've learned to cling to trauma, shame, and stress and grieve inward as a safe place. We believe that we guard our soul, spirit, and heart in clinging. Do we know, with our whole being, that it's ok to ask for help? Asking and receiving places us in an uncomfortable, vulnerable position.

God's breath and His work have never left His people. He provided the life of His Son, the sacrifice for the punishment we inherited from Adam. Death lost. Jesus breathed His Spirit on us. The breath of God, His Son's life, and the Spirit are for us and in us for all time. We abide, breathe, and rest as a branch grafted into the vine.

Jesus, the true vine, the root, provides our perfect, balanced home. We were cut away from the old and live a new life in Christ's life. Healing sap, the blood of Christ, flows freely to every cell of our body. The band-aid binds us in Him, together with one another. The vinedresser works continually to create balance—beautiful fruit and bountiful wine from our lives. We fix our eyes on Him. We breathe. We rest. We ask. We receive. We work the work He places before us.

STUDY 19: CONNECTING

"God, teach me more about connecting," flowed from my lips as I sat at the top of my driveway overlooking my vineyards. Day after day, year after year, I paused. I put my foot on my brake and stopped. Surveying our family property with wide-opened eyes, I prayed, "God, this land belongs to you. Please work through our land, through our vineyard and the vines, to connect people to your story, through our story."

Looking back, I can see that I loved and trusted God. I wanted to be close to Him and connect with others. The barrier to connection, however, was a deep chasm of shame, confusion, and isolation. "Disconnected" puts mildly the detached, disjointed world in which I lived. I presented myself to the world as a strong woman of God. Internally—heart, soul, spirit, mind, and emotions—terror gripped me. My internal, deep-seated beliefs included the certainty that God and others wouldn't love me if they knew me. This unhealthy belief kept me at arm's length from knowing myself!

Weary and worn down, I prayed for insight and wisdom. My prayers shifted to begging God to teach me to pray for myself. I implored God to send mature people of deep faith into my life to help me grow, balance, and bear the fruit of mature faith. My cousin, a strong man of faith reflected, "God's working in you so He can work through you!" God worked through Ron and Becki too.

I greeted Ron and Becki at the door of our newly opened wine-tasting room when they arrived for their scheduled Jesus Jeep tour. I asked, "Where is home for you?" "Chicago," they said as they glanced heavenward to the warm spring sky, reflecting, "It's winter at home." I bundled up in a coat for our outdoor tour. They wore light sweaters, commenting that 50 degrees felt just perfect!

They studied an old family photo hanging on the wall of the old blacksmith shop. Our family moved to Paso Robles, CA, from Geneseo, Illinois, a few hours west of their Chicago home. Waving my hand around our little museum, I said, "Each piece reflects an aspect of our seven-generation story." We quickly connected.

Our Jeep tour furthered our connection. We shared the word of God over the next hours as I talked about the vine and branches in my vineyard. They held the tiny little bud as I explained that the following year's growth was tightly wound up inside, visible only under a microscope. We paused in Paul's words in Ephesians 2:10, "For we are his workmanship, created in Christ Jesus for good works, which God prepared beforehand, that we should walk in them."

We touched the sap as it dripped from the wounded shoot and talked about the bright green colors inside the shoot I cut away. They watched me graft by cutting a slice into the rootstock and placing the branch in the wound. They gasped as I quietly said, "By His wounds we are healed" (1 Peter 2:24).

With eyes and hearts wide open, Ron and Becki listened to me tell the story of the vine through my vines while bouncing around in my Jeep. Training. Thinning. Pruning. Picking. Winemaking. I intently listened to them, too, as they shared Scripture with me.

At one point, I paused and said, "I can clearly see that every aspect of my vineyard connects to Jesus' words, I am the vine;

you are the branches. Abide. I've only scratched the surface of the rich connections, and I'm praying that God continues to reveal His word and work to me through my land." I continued, "In fact, I pray that prayer at the top of my driveway each time I return home."

I stood with Ron and Becki at my tasting room bar as they sipped tastes of Steinbeck wine. I thought about the fact that I hadn't really had a chance to look at their faces on our tour. We were busy looking at the vineyard and the vines. Their eyes reflected their hearts—filled with mercy and love for our story and our land. Their eyes and hearts drew me in. I took a chance at a deeper relationship with them. "I'm writing a book called *The Vine Speaks*.[3] A publisher asked me to unfold the concepts and Scripture verses we just shared. I've never written a book," I reflected.

Ron's visible excitement took me back. He said, "I work for a publishing company." Ron didn't say it then, but he is the senior vice president of Tyndale House Publishing. I swallowed hard as I recalled telling Ron and Becki a bit of my pain-filled divorce story. Dark emotions flooded my being, and I felt their eyes piercing my heart.

I was absolutely sure Ron would say, "You're broken and divorced. You shouldn't be writing a book!" Thoughts of pain, shame, distance, and brokenness flooded my mind in those few seconds. Overwhelmed by that moment of expectation, I forgot the beauty we had just shared on our Jesus Jeep tour.

---

3 The Vine Speaks St. Louis, MO, Concordia Publishing House. 2013.

In a very quiet, gentle voice, Ron said, "As a publisher, I've seen God work powerfully through the stories of very broken people." I swallowed hard. "Really," I blurted out, surprised at saying it out loud.

"Yes, Cindy," he continued. "People need hope. When they hear your story of God at work through your brokenness, they will trust that God can work in their story. Through your story, they see God's work."

Ron and Becki's eyes and words of mercy, Jesus' words of mercy through them, touched me deeply on that day. God answered my prayer by sending them to me to help me connect with faithful people. My story became more integrated because of their merciful words. And Jesus touched them deeply through my vines and wine. God connected us. God continues to work through our connection in Christ.

They've rejoiced with me over the years as God has faithfully worked healing in me and healing through me. They've urged me on, prayed with me, and cheered for me. They introduced me to their family and friends and allowed me to share their passion and pain.

Connecting with Beth Moore

Years later, Ron's text read, "Cindy, do you know Beth Moore?" "Well, I don't know her, but I certainly know who she is," I replied. Ron continued, "I'm her editor at Tyndale House Publishing, and I want to connect the two of you. Would you be willing to host Beth in Steinbeck Vineyards for the filming of the DVD for her new book *Chasing Vines*?"

Beth arrived on a hot Paso Robles day in early September 2019. Immediately she headed into the vineyard—I followed. Breathless in the beauty of the vines, she soaked in my words about the sap flow, the bud, the roots, and the fruit. Hungry to hear and learn, Beth declared, "I want you to tell me everything!"

Words flowed from my heart—grafted in Christ, abiding, bleeding, healing in Christ's wounds, and connected with one another.

Tears squirted from her beautiful eyes as she grabbed my forearm in sheer awe at the connections between the vines and Jesus, the true vine I'd made over the years. Jesus connected us through our mutual connection with Ron.

Beth and I enjoyed many moments alone as we bounced through my vineyard in my Jeep or walked through the vines. Beth and I each revealed bits of our pain-filled stories over those four wonderful days. We connected through mutual brokenness, but the hurt was not the focus of our conversations. We connected, most profoundly, through our healing journey in Christ. We shared awe and wonder of God's work through the vines, God's work in us, and God's work through us.

The Tyndale crew, the filming crew, Beth, Kimberly, and I stood in silence at the top of Oma's hill at the completion of the first morning's work. I slowly approached Beth and, in tears, asked, "May I give you a hug?" Inviting me toward her, she wondered about my deep emotion. I muttered, "I've been praying, begging God to work through our land for years. I never imagined He would work through it this way." She hugged me once again, praising God with me.

Beth invited me into her production. "Cindy," she directed, "speak your heart and passion for Christ, the true vine! Speak the story of the vinedresser's work grafting us into the vine. Speak the healing message you've learned in your vineyard."

"It's a wrap," declared the director after we filmed at Row 124. Beth hugged me tight, thanking me while I thanked her. Ron approached, in tears, and cried out, "This, this message—this is what Becki and I heard years ago. I connected the two of you for this very moment!"

Ron, Becki, Beth, and I connected through the healing word of God in my vineyard. God works through people, through writing, and through many varied means to connect us to one another.

Connecting the Word

Every day, the band-aid in my Bible draws my attention to connection—my connection with Adam, my connection to Christ, and our connection with one another. Adam's disobedience broke his and our intimate relationship with God. Christ restored the relationship and paved the way for us to be intimately connected to Him and to one another.

Meditate on the abiding connections made by Isaiah, Jesus, Peter, and Paul, connecting us to Christ's healing work.

Isaiah connected his hearers to Christ:

> For he grew up before him like a young plant, and like a root out of dry ground; he had no form or majesty that we should look at him, and no beauty that we should desire him. He was despised and rejected by men, a man of sorrows and acquainted with grief; and as one from whom

men hide their faces he was despised, and we esteemed him not. Isaiah 53:2-3

Jesus connected His work to Moses:

As Moses lifted up the serpent in the wilderness, so must the Son of Man be lifted up, that whoever believes in him may have eternal life. "For God so loved the world, that he gave his only Son, that whoever believes in him should not perish but have eternal life. For God did not send his Son into the world to condemn the world, but in order that the world might be saved through him. John 3:14-17

Do not think that I will accuse you to the Father. There is one who accuses you: Moses, on whom you have set your hope. For if you believed Moses, you would believe me; for he wrote of me. But if you do not believe his writings, how will you believe my words? John 5:45-47

Peter connected Isaiah's words to Jesus' work:

He was pierced for our transgressions; he was crushed for our iniquities; upon him was the chastisement that brought us peace, and with his wounds we are healed. Isaiah 53:5

He himself bore our sins in his body on the tree, that we might die to sin and live to righteousness. By his wounds you have been healed. 1 Peter 2:24

Paul made these profound connections:

> Therefore, just as sin came into the world through one man, and death through sin, and so death spread to all men because all sinned But the free gift is not like the trespass. For if many died through one man's trespass, much more have the grace of God and the free gift by the grace of that one man Jesus Christ abounded for many. And the free gift is not like the result of that one man's sin. For the judgment following one trespass brought condemnation, but the free gift following many trespasses brought justification. For if, because of one man's trespass, death reigned through that one man, much more will those who receive the abundance of grace and the free gift of righteousness reign in life through the one man Jesus Christ. Romans 5:12, 16-17

Powerful connections abound in the word of God. We are branches, cut away from the old, grafted into the life of the vine. The band-aid holds in place, reminding us of connectedness in Christ through the healing blood of Christ. The Spirit of Jesus keeps us in Him.

Connected IN Christ

Vineyard truths and images representing God's passionate work drive us toward deeper connection. Our response to connection flows from the vinedresser's work in us and through us. Be filled with holy awe and wonder at God's work through vineyard truths and imagery as you once again ponder these connections.

CREATION: God formed Adam, breathed into Adam, and Adam became a living being. God created vines and branches, knowing the rich truths dripping from sap and blood.

GRAFTED AND ROOTED: With a sharp knife and swift wound, the vinedresser grafted us into the life of the vine. We are held in our abiding place —the life of the holy, perfect, righteous root, by the Spirit. We dwell in Him, and He dwells in us.

TRELLIS AND TRAINING: God built the structure of life through the law. The law does not free us but supports us. His perfect Son obeyed every law perfectly. He willingly allowed His life to be sacrificed on our behalf. He trains us up in love, living in the life of His beloved Son.

THINNING AND PRUNING: The vinedresser positions shoots by thinning and pruning, so we might be more fruitful. Wounding by the hands of the vinedresser balances growth and the fruit we bear.

FRUIT AND HARVEST: The vinedresser works through our story, drawing from us the prime fruit of abiding. As we live and work, God provides a plethora of ways our prime fruit matures and works often, through extreme circumstances, to harvest the fruit of love and forgiveness.

WINE: Harvested fruit is crushed, fermented, and aged to perfection. The winemaker redeems every aspect of our lives as He crafts beautiful wine. He tastes the wine of our lives and declares it is good.

Responding to Connection

The fruit of connection matures and is harvested as we respond to being joined and attached to Jesus, the land, and to one another. Does our response to connection mirror the passion and breadth of God's pursuit of and work in us?

Does our response to being connected to Christ mirror the responses we see in the Scripture? Do we seek to understand the connection we share with one another grafted into Jesus' life? Do we seek to touch Him, fall on our faces and beg Him? Are we amazed? Do we follow? Once touched, do we touch others with Christ?

Images of people responding to Jesus' word and work as they brought their broken lives and their needs to Jesus provide a powerful witness. They were unashamed to be naked and in need before Him. Place yourself in these stories. Touch Jesus and beg Him to touch you. Respond to His call with zeal. Be amazed at His mercy and love. Follow His lead. Worship Jesus in the depth of your being.

> And he came down with them and stood on a level place, with a great crowd of his disciples and a great multitude of people from all Judea and Jerusalem and the seacoast of Tyre and Sidon, who came to hear him and to be healed of their diseases. And those who were troubled with unclean spirits were cured. All the crowd sought to touch him, for power came out from him and healed them all. Luke 6:17-19

> While he was in one of the cities, there came a man full

of leprosy. And when he saw Jesus, he fell on his face and begged him, "Lord, if you will, you can make me clean." And Jesus stretched out his hand and touched him, saying, "I will; be clean." And immediately the leprosy left him. Luke 5:12-13

Which is easier, to say, 'Your sins are forgiven you,' or to say, 'Rise and walk'? But that you may know that the Son of Man has authority on earth to forgive sins"—he said to the man who was paralyzed — "I say to you, rise, pick up your bed and go home." And immediately he rose up before them and picked up what he had been lying on and went home, glorifying God. Amazement seized them all, and they glorified God and were filled with awe, saying, "We have seen extraordinary things today." Luke 5:23-26

After this he went out and saw a tax collector named Levi, sitting at the tax booth. And he said to him, "Follow me." And leaving everything, he rose and followed him. Luke 5:27

He answered, "And who is he, sir, that I may believe in him?" Jesus said to him, "You have seen him, and it is he who is speaking to you." He said, "Lord, I believe," and he worshiped him. John 9:36-38

Response to connecting with Christ reflects our uniqueness in Christ. Some leap and praise God, and others bow quietly in grateful adoration. One person may run to Jesus with reckless abandon, another may walk cautiously toward Him. Others need friends to carry them into Jesus' loving arms.

Response to connecting with Christ varies as we pass through different stages of our journey. Some experience pain and sorrow so deep they didn't think they could take another step. At another time that same person jumped and laughed with great abandon. Much of life is lived right in the middle of those extremes. Through it all, we fix our eyes on Jesus, the author of our faith.

Longing for Connection

God breathed a holy longing into Adam's being as part of creating Adam in His image, and Adam passed them along to us. "So God created man in his own image, in the image of God he created him; male and female he created them" (Genesis 1:27). God longs for connection with us and with all people. The deep longing for connection binds us together with all people of all time. *All* people *want* connection; *all* people *need* connection.

Adam and Eve's attempts at connection, after they disobeyed God's one holy demand, provide insight into futile attempts we make to meet our need for connection apart from God. Hiding, blaming, lying, covering their nakedness—all were a flailing attempt to meet the deep craving for connection. They felt guilt and shame, anger and embarrassment, confusion and isolation for the first time in the history of the world. Is it any wonder that we struggle the way we do as we seek connection?

Asking ourselves these questions may give us insight into our need for connection. Are our moment-to-moment thoughts and actions grounded in our relationship with Christ? Do we attempt to meet our longings for balance, growing, healing, and connection through ways that hurt us or others?

God pursued Adam and Eve. God pursued and continues to pursue us. God made promises to them, and God made promises to us. God fulfilled promises in them, and He fulfills promises in us.

God sent Jesus into this world to connect people to Himself. The Word made flesh dwelled among the people. For three years, He gathered, He touched, and He healed. That profound work continues now, for us and in us. The word remains with us; the word dwells in us, and we live life grafted into Christ's life.

Faith says, "Amen" to the full and complete connection God worked in Christ. Connection with Christ provides a safe home in which we continue to learn how we process life and how we live.

Zero Degrees of Separation

We are only six degrees separated from anyone in the world, goes the theory. If you and I talked long enough, we would discover common acquaintances or friends. Fun conversations abound as we discover connections. If this is true, then why do many feel so alone and disconnected? Could it be that our way of thinking needs to be adjusted to reflect the truth of the word of God we're exploring?

Zero degrees of separation exist between you and Christ; zero degrees of separation exist between you and me in Christ! God's work and word connect us. We are intimately connected to Christ, to one another, to all people of all time, in all nations, and of all races.

*Zero degrees of separation exist
between you and me, in Christ!*

Being connected with Christ in Christ provides the place in which we balance, grow, heal, and bear fruit. Being connected in Christ, with zero degrees of separation, doesn't mean that I am the same as every other branch. Connectedness is not sameness. Each branch, while grafted into the one true vine, uniquely receives the work of the vinedresser. Each person individually heals and grows. Each of us bears unique fingerprints and distinct fruit of the story of our lives.

Christians, grafted into Christ, live forgiven and free together with us. Living in Christ, in relationships with others, provides plenty of opportunity to practice life-giving forgiveness and love. When we offend, we ask for forgiveness. When offended and the individual asks for forgiveness, we forgive. Love connects. Offending one another disconnects. Forgiveness reconnects.

We abide in Christ with zero degrees of separation. Jesus prayed for us and for all in the future who would be connected with Him through His testimony in and through our lives, "I do not ask for these only, but also for those who will believe in me through their word, that they may all be one, just as you, Father, are in me, and I in you, that they also may be in us, so that the world may believe that you have sent me" (John 17:20-21).

Connected in Christ with one another, we dwell in a safe home. His life provides our place of rest, an everlasting dwelling. Paul's words to the people of Philippi urge Christians to have the same mind, the mind of Christ. He calls them to tend unselfishly to their own needs and humbly to the needs of others as they abide in Christ.

> So if there is any encouragement in Christ, any comfort from love, any participation in the Spirit, any affection and sympathy, complete my joy by being of the same mind, having the same love, being in full accord and of one mind. Do nothing from selfish ambition or conceit, but in humility count others more significant than yourselves. Let each of you look not only to his own interests, but also to the interests of others. Philippians 2:1-4

STUDY 20: ABIDING

"Where is home for you?" I ask while launching our Jeep ride. Connecting with you is meaningful as we begin our time together. "This is my home," I state as I wave my hand toward the tan stucco home with barn-red window trim. "My Great Grandparents built this rambling vineyard home in 1921."

Imagine long days of work as great-grandma Rosie rekindled the warm coals of the old wood stove and cooked a hot breakfast before sunrise. Great-grandpa Frank fed and teamed up the horses to plow or harvest the fields. They'd partially unhitch and water the teams at noon, eat another big meal, and head back out to the fields.

By late afternoon teams fed quietly in the barn, resting for the next day's work. Supper took place around the family table set for 8—Frank, Rosie, their four rowdy boys, and my grandma Hazel, the middle child. Great, great-grandma, Barbara Amelia sat in the eighth spot. My father's fond memories and old photos continue to tell rich stories of love, practical jokes, music, and laughter.

Barbara Amelia spent her later years in an old rocking chair at my big picture window. She was well educated—theologically trained in Alsace Germany and a student of five languages, she read her old Bible daily and devoured any book she set eyes on. Dad recalls her tiny little body, eyes failing, rocking at the window, soaking up the morning sun. She'd hold the Bible close, even though she could barely make out the words on the pages.

The family Sunday routine included teaming up the horses, this time for a buggy ride to the old country church built by Frank's parents and uncles in 1885. They worshiped and then gathered back at the ranch house for an afternoon of music. My living room, I've been told, came alive with piano, violin, trumpet, and harmonica. Every family member played! Foot stomping and joyful music filled my home. Kids romped around outside while adults celebrated life inside. "Oh, If these walls could talk," I muse!

I know other stories, too, lesser told pain-filled stories. A second-born infant dying at birth. Brother against brother and parent against child. A child who loved music more than farming was ostracized. A grandmother raised a grandchild because of death and abandonment.

You probably know the stories because if your walls could talk, they'd tell similar stories.

Walls don't talk, and tragically, many families don't talk either. If families spoke matters of the heart with one another, in love, they would find a lot in common. They'd find coverups that include stories of shame, hiding, and blame. Looking good on the outside hides brokenness, or so we think. Not talking buries brokenness deep within the heart, spirit, and soul, creating a breeding ground for dis-connection, dis-ease, and depression.

Abiding IN Christ

The "walls" of our home in Christ speak! The word has spoken; the word speaks! He broke down walls of hostility between us and Him by obeying every command perfectly, by suffering, dying, and rising to new life. Paul proclaimed,

> But now in Christ Jesus you who once were far off have been brought near by the blood of Christ. For he himself is our peace, who has made us both one and has broken down in his flesh the dividing wall of hostility by abolishing the law of commandments expressed in ordinances, that he might create in himself one new man in place of the two, so making peace, and might reconcile us both to God in one body through the cross, thereby killing the hostility. Ephesians 2:13-16

Abide, as we've discussed, means to live, remain, stay, dwell, reside, to continue in a particular attitude or relationship. To abide is to be. We dwell safely in Christ, secure in His love. We're invited into a quiet, internal calm, filled with peace. Abiding IN Christ provides a home in which to balance, grow, heal, and connect.

> Then justice will dwell in the wilderness, and righteousness abide in the fruitful field. And the effect of righteousness will be peace, and the result of righteousness, quietness and trust forever. My people will abide in a peaceful habitation, in secure dwellings, and in quiet resting places. Isaiah 32:16-18

Christ spoke, "Abide in me," amid turmoil to eleven confused followers. At the conclusion of Jesus' "I am" statement and the images He drew with vines and branches, Jesus told them, "I have said all these things to you to keep you from falling away" (John 16:1). In a few hours, they would scatter. John recorded Jesus saying,

> Behold, the hour is coming, indeed it has come, when you will be scattered, each to his own home, and will leave me alone. Yet I am not alone, for the Father is with me. I have said these things to you, that in me you may have peace. In the world you will have tribulation. But take heart; I have overcome the world. John 16:32-33

Take heart; I have overcome the world.

Jesus' life provides, fully and completely, the security and rest we deeply crave. Peace and joy flow, not from an earthly home or wealth, but from life in Christ. Joy-filled people around the world, many of whom live homeless in poverty know their home, their abiding place. They live in Jesus. Their earthly needs may not be met, but heir home is secure and complete. Jesus is light, living water, bread, the shepherd, the way, the truth, and their life. Quietness and peace flow from their grateful hearts. Their faces radiate hope and love amid severe trials.

Christ Dwelling in You and Me

While journeying toward the cross, Jesus spoke,

> Abide in me, and I in you. As the branch cannot bear fruit by itself, unless it abides in the vine, neither can you, unless you abide in me. I am the vine; you are the branches. Whoever abides in me and I in him, he it is that bears much fruit, for apart from me you can do nothing. John 15:4-5

The bulk of our study has drawn our attention to Jesus, our

abiding place, as a branch to the vine. We must not overlook the fact that twice, in two powerful sentences, Jesus says, "Abide in me, and I in you!" John recorded Jesus' powerful words that preceded His call to abide: "If anyone loves me, he will keep my word, and my Father will love him, and we will come to him and make our home with him" (John 14:23).

"We will make our home with him," proclaimed Jesus. The Triune God dwells in us! Paul invites us to wrap our faith around these words, "That Christ may dwell in your hearts through faith—that you, being rooted and grounded in love" (Ephesians 3:17). Jesus promised to dwell in our hearts through faith. Jesus did not promise to dwell in our heads through faith.

> *Jesus promised to dwell in our hearts through faith, not our heads.*

The temptation to stay in our heads with matters of the heart affects all people. We attempt to make sense of the senseless, neatly categorize messes, and by doing so, bury our hungry souls. Christ, abiding in us, invites us into His work in His way. Our way attempts to keep our relationship with Jesus neat and tidy. Jesus' way summons, "follow me."

The blind man's story (John 9) captures every beautifully messy, powerfully poignant piece of the work and word of Jesus Christ. Put your story into this story. The man's blindness stimulated questions about illness and sin. Maybe we've asked a similar question as we've tried to make sense of pain and brokenness. "Rabbi, who sinned, this man or his parents, that he was born blind?" Jesus answered, "It was not that this man sinned, or his parents, but that the works of God might be displayed in him" (John 9:2-3).

The blind man could not see Jesus, but he certainly heard Him spitting and making mud. He felt Jesus pack a mud pie on his blind eyes. He followed Jesus' command to go and wash. He returned with 20-20 vision. Religious leaders, whom he had never seen, grilled him for answers to explain how his sight was restored.

This story may be our story—do we squash our journey just to stay within religious boundaries? Dare we talk about healing and balance, risking being branded "new agers?" Are we brave enough to beg God to integrate all aspects of our being? Are we so bold as to believe God wants us to live life apart from abusive, hurtful people?

Religious leaders threw the healed man out of the church. Jesus approached the ostracized man, the formerly blind man who had not yet seen Him. Jesus asked, "Do you believe in the man who packed a mud pie on your eyes?" Jesus' question reflected His quiet invitation, "Abide in me and I in you." Right there, right then, the man who had been thrown out of his place of worship worshiped Jesus.

The blind man knew his need; the contrite and lowly knew their need for Jesus. Isaiah declared, "For thus says the One who is high and lifted up, who inhabits eternity, whose name is Holy: 'I dwell in the high and holy place, and also with him who is of a contrite and lowly spirit, to revive the spirit of the lowly, and to revive the heart of the contrite'" (Isaiah 57:15).

Our blindness falls away as we trust Jesus' invitation and

work for us and in us. Control fades, and we are bold to proclaim, "I abide in Christ; Christ abides in me." "Thy will be done on earth, in me, as it is in heaven," we boldly pray. His abiding work for us and in us leads to Christ at work through us, through our stories.

Christ at Work Through Me and You

The temptation to perfect our story prior to God working affects us all. As you've witnessed from my story, God works through pain, suffering, and brokenness to heal.

You've been wounded, and you've suffered, too. God works through your wounds and your pain to harvest the fruit of forgiveness and love. He faithfully forgives your desire to hold on to someone's hurtful actions. As you plunk your pain in Row 124, God heals. Christ works in you. He profoundly desires connection with you as He redeems you and your whole story. And Christ works through you to shine light into darkness.

Before the foundation of the world, God loved Jesus. Jesus is our eternal home, prayed, "Father, I desire that they also, whom you have given me, may be with me where I am, to see my glory that you have given me because you loved me before the foundation of the world" (John 17:24). Jesus holds us in His very body—our abiding place, our dwelling place. Being held in His life includes eternity both past and future.

Paul's profound words call us to bow before the vinedresser and the vine in humble awe at His work. The very same power of God, the power of God that raised Jesus from the dead, works in us. I imagine Paul standing on his tiptoes, proclaiming this truth:

> I do not cease to give thanks for you, remembering you in my prayers, that the God of our Lord Jesus Christ, the Father of glory, may give you the Spirit of wisdom and of revelation in the knowledge of him, having the eyes of your hearts enlightened, that you may know what is the hope to which he has called you, what are the riches of his glorious inheritance in the saints, and what is the immeasurable greatness of his power toward us who believe, according to the working of his great might that he worked in Christ when he raised him from the dead and seated him at his right hand in the heavenly places, far above all rule and authority and power and dominion, and above every name that is named, not only in this age but also in the one to come. And he put all things under his feet and gave him as head over all things to the church, which is his body, the fullness of him who fills all in all. Ephesians 1:16-23

God breathed His breath into us. God's call invites us to grow and live as fully alive human beings!

On a May day in 2020, Steve and I, as dear friends, were walking and talking in my vineyard. As we spoke, he said, "I'm just not ready to date. I don't want to get to know someone from scratch. Someone from church wants me to go out with this lady whose husband passed away." I swallowed and took the courage to say, "If your heart is ever ready to date, I have someone in mind."

He asked, "who?" We stopped. I said, "me." We spoke of this again in July when we saw one another. By August, he had asked and received his kids' blessing. We were engaged in December and married in February 2021.

Ah, perfection, even though we chose to commute between San Diego and Paso Robles until Steve retired. I began noticing health issues. The first symptoms were a swollen finger and unusual pain in my feet and hands. Eventually, after a year and a half of doctors and tests, I was diagnosed with Multiple Myeloma.

My body was failing me. The physical symptoms included extreme weight loss, severe muscle stiffness, and bone pain. I bruised easily, and I couldn't rest enough. I wasn't able to play with my grandkids. Discouragement set in as I became weak and frail.

Christ's healing blood never fails. I fixed my eyes on Him. My hope rested on God's promise of complete reconciliation through the perfect blood of Christ. The images of my life, grafted into Christ's holy life, and the healing sap flow kept me moving forward. God worked through modern medicine.

The medication worked beautifully, and I quickly began to feel healthy again. Then the doctor said, "we want you to explore stem cell transplant." While exciting, we were scared, and for good reason. Steve's wife of 19 years, Joyce, was diagnosed with leukemia in July 2016. She underwent aggressive treatment including chemo and radiation. Eventually, a bone marrow donor was located.

Her transplant took place in November 2016. In her weakened state, she got an infection that her body could not fight. Her body failed, and she met Jesus face-to-face a few short weeks after her transplant. Her words to Steve before being intubated were, "when I wake up, my numbers are going to be perfect." He watched from the sidelines as doctors attempted to revive her. In a moment, she was gone. Her numbers were perfect when she woke in Jesus' arms, face to face with Him.

Steve deeply grieved his loss while rejoicing that Joyce was no longer suffering. Vowing never to love another so deeply, he grieved. He allowed me into his journey as his friend. Dare I pray that Steve could or ever would love me? Dare I ask God to heal his heart to make room to love? Tentatively I did, and then more boldly, I asked God. Friends prayed too and God answered those prayers. And now, we were faced, five years later, with a blood cancer similar in nature to Joyce's leukemia.

As we studied and listened to doctors, we agreed to the stem cell transplant. We also learned terms such as harvesting and grafting from the medical perspective. My cells have been harvested and put back into my bloodstream. They returned to my bone marrow and "grafted" into their former home. I have a new birthday—October 25, 2022. I received a new immune system through my stem cells on that day.

We continue to be in awe as my body recovers, thankful for my new life. We thank God for the UCLA doctors and teams of researchers who discovered stem cell treatment as a cure for Multiple Myeloma. Living each day *in* Christ propels me forward in His healing mercy. Redeemed and reconciled to God through the blood of Christ drives my every breath on this earth, for however many moments I have to live in my body. My body will fail me again, someday. Redeemed and reconciled to God through Christ's blood gives me hope today and an unshakeable eternal hope.

Jesus Is Holding You

My dear friend Janine lay bedridden. She beat breast cancer once before, but not this time. As I lay with her, holding her, praying with her, I knew it would be the last time I would see her on this earth.

Janine was a master teacher, loved by all. Her husband died in a military helicopter crash when their daughter was only six months old. Janine raised her beautiful daughter as a faithful single mom.

My prayer lasted for what seemed like an eternity. I couldn't bring myself to stop. My "amen" led to slowly releasing our embrace. I gazed into her peace-filled eyes and quietly whispered, "Janine, just know Jesus is holding you."

She confidently and, without hesitation, replied, "I know He is because you are!" Janine held me, and I held her on that painful, beautiful day in 2005. Janine's voice spoke Jesus to me, and I spoke Jesus to her. Her profound words permeated the depth of my being.

You and I hold the holy privilege of being Jesus' hands, feet, heart, and voice. He also invites us to allow those around us, safe people, to hold us as we journey in this life. As we abide in Him and He in us, we reflect His love and mercy in this world.

STUDY 21: MULTIPLYING GROWTH

Multiplication can be seen everywhere in the vineyard and winery! Dormant pruned vines spring forth with new growth in March. Visible fruit forms burst open in May, pollinating and setting the fruit for the growing season. Yeast multiplies on freshly picked and processed grapes in our winemaking facility, creating the fermentation we need to make wine.

Inexperienced winemakers often make a rookie mistake by overfilling a fermentation vat. As yeast works, it creates heat and expansion. Overly full vats overflow as the fermenting grapes expand! Good juice runs down the drain because of multiplication.

Multiplication takes place in challenging ways too. Deer multiply, creating unending challenges to our grape-growing operation. Outbreaks of unwanted bugs create threats to our operation. Weeds multiply exponentially too!

Our Steinbeck wine label has multiplied. We began processing our own fruit in 2006. We crushed a few tons of grapes in order to make a couple of hundred cases of wine. In 2022 we crush over 30 tons, and we're approaching 2,000 cases of wine. We've grown our wine brand because our customer base has expanded. Customers hear and love our story and our wine. They tell others. Growth multiplies.

Our family multiplied. My son Ryan, sixth generation vinedresser, married Caitlin. They gave me two grandchildren, Bradley and Amelia. My daughter, Stacy, married Bryan. They have three children Joryn, Allora, and Cyrus.

Multiplying Mercy; Multiplying Hate

Jesus worked and works exponentially. Jesus' words multiplied mercy; Jesus' words multiplied hate. The authors of the Gospels made this abundantly clear as they testified to the work of the Messiah. Every story contains an element of multiplication.

Jesus touched a leper, an unclean man, and made him whole. Great crowds gathered according to this first account from Luke's gospel. In the second story, we see religious leaders filled with fury. Luke reflected that Jesus knew their thoughts—exponential thoughts of hatred toward Jesus. Jesus' work created exponential thoughts of love and a deep desire to be in the presence of Jesus in those who followed Jesus. The work of God through Jesus created disdain and a desire to rid the world of Jesus for those who rejected the Lord of life. Every account of Jesus' word and action breeds an exponential component of mercy or hate.

> While he was in one of the cities, there came a man full of leprosy. And when he saw Jesus, he fell on his face and begged him, "Lord, if you will, you can make me clean." And Jesus stretched out his hand and touched him, saying, "I will; be clean." And immediately the leprosy left him. And he charged him to tell no one, but "go and show yourself to the priest, and make an offering for your cleansing, as Moses commanded, for a proof to them." But now even more the report about him went abroad, and great crowds gathered to hear him and to be healed of their infirmities.
> Luke 5:12-15

> On another Sabbath, he entered the synagogue and was teaching, and a man was there whose right hand was withered. And the scribes and the Pharisees watched him, to see whether he would heal on the Sabbath, so that they might find a reason to accuse him. But he knew their thoughts, and he said to the man with the withered hand, "Come and stand here." And he rose and stood there. And Jesus said to them, "I ask you, is it lawful on the Sabbath to do good or to do harm, to save life or to destroy it?" And after looking around at them all he said to him, "Stretch out your hand." And he did so, and his hand was restored. But they were filled with fury and discussed with one another what they might do to Jesus. Luke 6:6-11

Matthew revealed the multiplication of Jesus' mercy by inviting, "Come to me, all who labor and are heavy laden, and I will give you rest. Take my yoke upon you, and learn from me, for I am gentle and lowly in heart, and you will find rest for your souls. For my yoke is easy, and my burden is light" (Matthew 11:28-30).

Matthew summarized the multiplication of the religious leader's hate this way, "For John came neither eating nor drinking, and they say, 'He has a demon.' The Son of Man came eating and drinking, and they say, 'Look at him! A glutton and a drunkard, a friend of tax collectors and sinners!' Yet wisdom is justified by her deeds" (Matthew 11:18-19).

What are we to do with the fact that when Jesus walked this earth His actions multiplied mercy or hate? If we read these accounts and our hearts are not stirred by the polarizing multiplying nature of the Gospel are we really hearing with our hearts?

Hearts are either softened or hardened, there is no lukewarm.

The Son of God walked this earth, doing the work His father sent Him to accomplish for us. Jesus, one man loved by those who received his message, hated by many, walked the lonely journey through suffering and to the cross alone. He lay lifeless in the grave, alone. His father raised Him alone, from the dead. Jesus' resurrection sealed the work of God through Him, for us and for all.

Evidence of the exponential growth of the Gospel of Jesus Christ, by the power of the Holy Spirit, is right in front of us— He called you and me. We abide in Him, and He is in us. Is there any difference between our hearts being stirred by Jesus' work and Jesus' followers immediately following Jesus' resurrection?

Luke recorded the story and Peter's Spirit-filled words in Acts 4. Guards arrested Peter and John because they healed a man who had been crippled from birth and because they proclaimed Jesus' resurrection from the dead. "As they were speaking to the people, the priests and the captain of the temple and the Sadducees came upon them, greatly annoyed because they were teaching the people and proclaiming in Jesus the resurrection from the dead" (Acts 4:1-2).

Peter's message revealed the exponential nature of mercy and hate. Religious leaders put Jesus to death and then tried to cover up His resurrection through those who guarded Jesus' tomb.

> While they were going, behold, some of the guard went into the city and told the chief priests all that had taken place. And when they had assembled with the elders and taken counsel, they gave a sufficient sum of money to

the soldiers and said, "Tell people, 'His disciples came by night and stole him away while we were asleep.' And if this comes to the governor's ears, we will satisfy him and keep you out of trouble." So they took the money and did as they were directed. And this story has been spread among the Jews to this day. Matthew 28:11-15

The high-priestly family's orders to Peter were clear, "'In order that it may spread no further among the people, let us warn them to speak no more to anyone in this name.' So they called them and charged them not to speak or teach at all in the name of Jesus" (Acts 4:18). Prior to this order, Peter proclaimed:

> Then Peter, filled with the Holy Spirit, said to them, "Rulers of the people and elders, if we are being examined today concerning a good deed done to a crippled man, by what means this man has been healed, let it be known to all of you and to all the people of Israel that by the name of Jesus Christ of Nazareth, whom you crucified, whom God raised from the dead—by him this man is standing before you well. This Jesus is the stone that was rejected by you, the builders, which has become the cornerstone. And there is salvation in no one else, for there is no other name under heaven given among men by which we must be saved." Acts 4:8-12

Peter and John, filled with the Holy Spirit, answered their order this way: "Whether it is right in the sight of God to listen to you rather than to God, you must judge, for we cannot but speak of what we have seen and heard" (Acts 4:19-20). Filled with the Holy Spirit, we cannot but speak of what we have seen and heard. We grow in the one true vine, embracing and sharing the redemption and reconciliation that is ours in Christ. Life in Christ, and Christ in us, guide our listening and speaking, our hearts and minds.

Multiplying Wisdom

The Scriptures proclaim Jesus, as the wisdom of God and Jesus calls Himself the wisdom of God. Luke recorded that while speaking to the Pharisees and lawyers, Jesus declared,

> Therefore also the Wisdom of God said, 'I will send them prophets and apostles, some of whom they will kill and persecute,' so that the blood of all the prophets, shed from the foundation of the world, may be charged against this generation from the blood of Abel to the blood of Zechariah, who perished between the altar and the sanctuary. Yes, I tell you, it will be required of this generation. Woe to you lawyers! For you have taken away the key of knowledge. You did not enter yourselves, and you hindered those who were entering. Luke 11:49-52

The apostle Paul clearly understood Jesus as the wisdom of God and calls us into a deeper understanding of the wisdom that is ours in Jesus. We are wise to rest in Paul's words as we grow in our understanding of the gift of wisdom, the gift of Jesus.

> For Jews demand signs and Greeks seek wisdom, but we preach Christ crucified, a stumbling block to Jews and folly to Gentiles, but to those who are called, both

> Jews and Greeks, Christ the power of God and the wisdom of God. For the foolishness of God is wiser than men, and the weakness of God is stronger than men. 1 Corinthians 1:22-25

> God chose what is low and despised in the world, even things that are not, to bring to nothing things that are, so that no human being might boast in the presence of God. And because of him you are in Christ Jesus, who became to us wisdom from God, righteousness and sanctification and redemption, so that, as it is written, "Let the one who boasts, boast in the Lord." 1 Corinthians 1:28-31

Paul's words encourage us further through these words to the Christians two thousand years ago, "That their hearts may be encouraged, being knit together in love, to reach all the riches of full assurance of understanding and the knowledge of God's mystery, which is Christ, in whom are hidden all the treasures of wisdom and knowledge" (Colossians 2:2-3).

> For this reason, because I have heard of your faith in the Lord Jesus and your love toward all the saints, I do not cease to give thanks for you, remembering you in my prayers, that the God of our Lord Jesus Christ, the Father of glory, may give you the Spirit of wisdom and of revelation in the knowledge of him, having the eyes of your hearts enlightened, that you may know what is the hope to which he has called you, what are the riches of his glorious inheritance in the saints, and what is the immeasurable greatness of his power toward us who believe, according

to the working of his great might that he worked in Christ when he raised him from the dead and seated him at his right hand in the heavenly places, far above all rule and authority and power and dominion, and above every name that is named, not only in this age but also in the one to come. Ephesians 1:15-21

The very power of God that raised Jesus from the dead works the multiplication of Himself in us and through us. His Spirit of wisdom and revelation in the knowledge of Him works in our hearts and minds growing our wisdom and our faith. He multiplies our influence too.

Multiplying Influence

The terroir into which we were born partially defines our influence. Our influence multiplies as we grow in our understanding of ourselves and the world around us. How do we grow in wisdom and understanding? Why would people listen? Christ Jesus, the very wisdom of God, in the flesh, multiplies His wisdom in us. Our wisdom multiplies as He multiplies in us. The wisdom of God manifests in Jesus the true vine. We dwell in the vine, and He dwells in us. Every aspect of our being is touched—spiritual, physical, and emotional.

Be curious. Ask questions. Have we stopped asking questions? Are we satisfied knowing what we know? Do we place ourselves at the feet of Jesus, reflecting on His questions of us?

Think about how we think. Are we satisfied with our own thoughts? Are we willing to reflect on our thoughts and grow in maturity?

Fellowship with wise Christians. Do we seek out relationships with people who will raise our self-awareness and challenge our faith walk?

Expand knowledge by reading experts. What are our growth goals? Do they include sitting at the feet of experts in a wide variety of subjects?

Immerse in the Scriptures. Do I read the Scriptures, looking for what I already know? Do I sit at wisdom's feet, asking Him to reveal His work in me?

Work on our whole being—body, mind, heart, spirit. Do I exercise my body? Do I exercise my mind? Do I exercise my heart and spirit? Do I take care of my whole being?

We gave our former winemaker, Steve, the green light on this request, "please let me craft a blend for you out of your top barrels." We called the wine The VOICE. The name VOICE is significant—the vinedresser, my Dad Howie, farmed his whole career and never marketed his premium grapes. Additionally, music plays a significant role in our past and present. The most significant meaning, however, is the VOICE of the Scriptures and our voice.

Steve initially crafted three barrels equalling 72 cases of VOICE. Why 72? Jesus, the One, sent 12 into the harvest, and Jesus sent 72 into the harvest (Luke 10). We are beneficiaries of Jesus' voice, connected *in* Christ with the fruit of the life of Jesus and the voices of the 12 and the 72. That is how the Gospel multiplies—one to twelve to seventy-two. We have heard the voice of wisdom; we speak wisdom.

Jesus, the wisdom of God declared,

Truly, truly, I say to you, whoever hears my word and believes him who sent me has eternal life. He does not come into judgment, but has passed from death to life. Truly, truly, I say to you, an hour is coming, and is now here, when the dead will hear the voice of the Son of God, and those who hear will live. John 5:24-25

We have heard the voice of the vinedresser and the vine. Through His Spirit we receive, we grow, and we speak the word of truth to those with whom we have influence. Through His word and through us He works to multiply His love in this world.

May God continue to bless your journey — resting, growing, and healing in the life of the one true vine.

TERMS & CONCEPTS

Aging wine. Wine is placed in containers, oak barrels for the reds, and stainless steel for the whites. Our red wines age for eighteen months to two years before being bottled. The whites and roses are aged for six months to a year and then bottled.

Balance. A critical aspect in growing prime fruit—the shoots in the canopy must be grown evenly and the fruit must be in proportion to the canopy growth for optimum color, acid, and ripening. A critical aspect in making premium wine—color, tannins, acidity must be in harmony.

Bi-lateral. A type of trellis system where two canes are trained and grow in two directions from the trunk.

Branch. For our study, the branch protrudes from the graft union, about three inches above the soil. That branch grows and is trained as the trunk and then trained onto the cordon wire. Shoots grow from the branch and bear fruit.

Graft Union

Bud. At every leaf, a small bud protrudes laterally. It contains fruit and canopy growth for the following year.

Canopy. Shoots and leaves shade the fruit while allowing sunlight to filter onto the fruit.

Cordon. Horizontal shoots, often trained bi-laterally, that is tied to the training wire and remains year after year.

Cross section. Slicing a bud with a razor blade and placing a small sample of the inner part of the bud under a microscope reveals the growth for the following year.

Fermentation. Yeast combined with natural sugars from the fruit creates heat, converting natural sugars to alcohol. This process takes place over a two to three week period in our wine processing facility.

Graft. A bud cut off of a shoot is placed into the flesh of our chosen rootstock. The sliced bud and the like sized cut in the rootstock match perfectly. Those grafting place a bandaid like substance around the rootstock and bud to hold them together until healing takes place.

Graft union. The place where the bud and the rootstock are joined as one.

Harvest. The flurry of activity picking ripe fruit and sending it to be processed. We generally harvest the last week of August through the end of October.

Grafter's hands slicing into rootstock, making a "home" for the bud (branch)

Prime fruit. Fruit grows in varying sizes. The largest clusters are the prime fruit.

Prime shoots. Shoots grow from the buds on cordon, potentially three from each bud. The strongest is left on the cordon while the other two smaller, weaker are taken off through shoot thinning.

Prune. During the winter months growth from the previous year is trimmed back significantly, leaving two buds per spur rising up from the cordon. Cutting away good buds to position growth.

Spurs rising up from cordon

Ripe fruit. Random samples are taken in field blocks regularly leading up to harvest in order to check sugars, color and acidity. We pick wine grapes at about 25 percent sugar.

Roots. The all-important underground part of the grapevine that provides stability and absorbed nutrients and water from the soil. The roots are often ten feet deep with the feeder roots in the top ten inches of soil.

Sap flows to open wound and forms a healing scab

Bud on spur opening up—shoots and fruit beginning to burst forth in spring

Rootstock. A disease resistant grapevine that doesn't produce fruit is chosen based upon our soils and climate. The bud is grafted onto the root and grows up as a varietal vine such as cabernet sauvignon. The rootstock provides the host home for the life of the plant.

Sap. Fluid that circulates at all times to every cell within walls of the entire plant. Visible bleeding takes place during the spring when a wound is created by pruning.

Shoots. Also known as canes, shoots grow from buds developed the previous year. Leaves and fruit grow on shoots.

Spurs. Rising up from the cordon, spurs contain buds that burst forth in new growth in the spring.

Prime fruit at harvest

Tannin. A natural product extracted from grapes skins and seeds that brings structure and aging potential to wine.

Jeep ride in Steinbeck Vineyards

Tasting Room. Customers gather to taste our wines and enjoy the stories from our museum-like gathering place.

Terroir. A sense of place—the land, our farming practices, weather, and all factors contributing to the uniqueness of Paso Robles and Steinbeck Vineyards.

Thinning shoots and fruit. A hands-on process that cleans excess growth, leaving prime shoots and fruit for the current growing season. Prepares vineyard for pruning the following winter.

Train. To guide growth of trunk, cordon, and canopy by tying to wires.

Training wire. One wire is dedicated to the cordon as it is trained. The cordon remains tied to the training wire for the life of the vine.

Trellis system. The structure upon which branches, shoots, canes are trained. The wire and metal structure supports the weight of the fruit.

Trunk. Point above graft union, growing upward. For our imagery, the trunk is the beginning of the branch.

Steinbeck Wines

Vinedresser. One who cares for and tends vines. Can include wine making and tending vines.

Vineyard. The whole. On our land, Steinbeck Vineyards, we grow over 400 acres of wine grapes. We harvest approximately 2% of our crop for Steinbeck wine, the remaining crop is sold to large producers who market and sell their wines nationally.

The "Jesus" Vine
discovered by Leslie in 2013 (31 years old)
Photo: Richard Baker Painting: Al Weingartner

Cindy & Steve February 2021

Made in United States
Troutdale, OR
10/30/2024